THE GREATEST SPY WRITERS OF THE 20TH CENTURY

THE GREATEST SPY WRITERS OF THE 20TH CENTURY

BUCHAN, FLEMING AND LE CARRÉ

PHIL CARRADICE

PEN & SWORD HISTORY

AN IMPRINT OF PEN & SWORD BOOKS LTD.
YORKSHIRE – PHILADELPHIA

First published in Great Britain in 2023 by
PEN AND SWORD HISTORY
An imprint of
Pen & Sword Books Ltd
Yorkshire – Philadelphia

Copyright © Phil Carradice, 2023

ISBN 978 1 39907 186 4

The right of Phil Carradice to be identified as Author of this work has been asserted by her in accordance with the Copyright, Designs and Patents Act 1988.

A CIP catalogue record for this book is available from the British Library.

All rights reserved. No part of this book may be reproduced or transmitted in any form or by any means, electronic or mechanical including photocopying, recording or by any information storage and retrieval system, without permission from the Publisher in writing.

Typeset in Times New Roman 12/16 by
SJmagic DESIGN SERVICES, India.
Printed and bound in the UK by CPI Group (UK) Ltd.

Pen & Sword Books Limited incorporates the imprints of Atlas, Archaeology, Aviation, Discovery, Family History, Fiction, History, Maritime, Military, Military Classics, Politics, Select, Transport, True Crime, Air World, Frontline Publishing, Leo Cooper, Remember When, Seaforth Publishing, The Praetorian Press, Wharncliffe Local History, Wharncliffe Transport, Wharncliffe True Crime and White Owl.

For a complete list of Pen & Sword titles please contact
PEN & SWORD BOOKS LIMITED
George House, Units 12 & 13, Beevor Street, Off Pontefract Road,
Barnsley, South Yorkshire, S71 1HN, England
E-mail: enquiries@pen-and-sword.co.uk
Website: www.pen-and-sword.co.uk

or
PEN AND SWORD BOOKS
1950 Lawrence Rd, Havertown, PA 19083, USA
E-mail: uspen-and-sword@casematepublishers.com
Website: www.penandswordbooks.com

Contents

Dedication	vi
Acknowledgements	viii
Introduction	ix

Chapter One	Making a Choice; the Birth of Spy Fiction	1
Chapter Two	John Buchan, a Child of the Kirk	23
Chapter Three	From the Veldt to Border Hunting	35
Chapter Four	A World of Spies	52
Chapter Five	Ian Fleming, Bond Alive	67
Chapter Six	A Good War	81
Chapter Seven	Bond, Alive and Kicking	93
Chapter Eight	A Modest Little Secret Agent	113
Chapter Nine	Smiley Takes the Prize	125
Chapter Ten	The Triumvirate on the Silver Screen – and More	136

Notes	146
Bibliography	149

Dedication

This book is dedicated to the memory of my grandfather, Robert Turnbull Carradice. He was the wise grandparent who, at the beginning of a glorious four-week summer holiday at his home outside Barnard Castle, presented me with a copy of *Huntingtower* and suggested that I might like to read it. I was nine years old at the time and spent the next three days with my nose pressed to the book. *Huntingtower* was, I thought, a fascinating read, a feeling or emotion that has never left me.

Next in granddad's book selection came *The Thirty-Nine Steps* along with his advice that if I could persevere enough to make it through Chapter One the rest would more than compensate. He was right and when, later in that same memorable holiday, we drove out into the wilds of the Scottish borders Richard Hannay came alive in my imagination as I crawled and ran through the heather. Wonderful.

Years later, just a few weeks before he died, I was able to return the favour when I presented him with a copy of *The Spy Who Came in from the Cold*. The book had just come out and would, I hoped appeal to my grandfather's tastes. He had lost his power of speech by then but over the next week I watched him devour the text and the day before he was admitted to hospital for the final time, he held up le Carré's tome, smiled and gave me the thumbs up. I cherish the moment, sad though it may be.

I had already tried to interest him in the James Bond novels which I was then enjoying. He steadfastly refused to be drawn, whispering that they were fine for young people but not for him. Later, after his death, I found a copy of *From Russia with Love* on his bedside chair where he kept all the books he was reading or intending to read.

Dedication

I don't know if he had read it but I hope he managed to do so in the short time he had left to him.

Thanks, Granddad, for all the years of enjoyment and pleasure. Thanks for the guidance.

Acknowledgements

My father, grandfather and, indeed, all of my family, for whom the books and heroes of John Buchan were always alive

Deb Fisher who proof-read the MS – an onerous job at the best of times, nearly impossible with my MS

My darling Trudy, always at my shoulder, always missed

Introduction

Spying, they say, is the second oldest profession in the world – leaving you in little or no doubt as to which is the oldest one! That being the case, it remains a wonder that the art of writing spy or espionage fiction is such a relatively new phenomenon.

As you will see if you continue reading, the spy novel is really little more than a hundred years old. Yet in that brief enclave between its inception and the present day it has become one of the most popular forms of literary endeavour, both for the readers and for writers. Most of us will have read at least one spy novel, be it Ian Fleming's Bond, Len Deighton's more low-key adventures or any of the countless alternative offerings.

Writers like Graham Greene, Eric Ambler and Somerset Maugham have all contributed to the genre. But deciding who is the best – if such a word can be used to describe any piece of literature or any specific writer – leaves you with a quandary which may or may not be filled in the following pages of this book.

At the end of the day, it inevitably comes down to personal preference, your own preferences, your own likes and dislikes. And yet there are certain writers who hold a seminal position in the art of writing espionage thrillers. They may or may not be the best writers, per se, but they are magnificent proponents of an art form which has become increasingly popular.

In hindsight, it is almost impossible to separate spy fiction from spy fact. The first decade and a half of the twentieth century was a time of fear and apprehension as the great powers of Europe began flexing their muscles and coveting positions of control. Governments – the British government in particular – became desperate to know what other powers were doing, the extent of their military strength and so on. Hence the growth of spying as a profession. And as spies began to proliferate, spy literature grew in size and importance along with its real-life counterpart.

The Great War saw the defeat of Kaiser Wilhelm's Germany and the re-establishing of some form of status quo but spying was certainly not dead in the water. The 1920s and '30s brought the growth of the German Nazi Party, the Russian resurgence after the Revolution of 1917 and fear of what might happen in the world. With that fear of what developments might lead to, anxiety and the need to know what was happening behind 'closed doors' became rampant once again.

Defeat of Hitler in 1945 did not bring universal peace. Instead, it brought fear of the one great outburst which just might destroy everything. The Cold War period of the 1950s and '60s saw the same old problem, the same result. Arguably, the Cold War – when the world was at its most vulnerable – saw the greatest ever proliferation of good quality spy fiction. And that intense flowering of espionage writing has not yet gone away.

I am convinced of one thing – any study of the great spy writers can only help readers in their enjoyment of the genre. What follows here offers readers an option – you can agree or disagree as you read about the three writers who I have called The Triumvirate. Sounds like one of James Bond's enemy organisations, doesn't it?

Read the book, then go back to your own choices if you like. But perhaps you might find time to spare a thought about The Triumvirate or any of the other writers I have mentioned. Or, for that matter, those I have not! Read on, Macduff – as the bard did *not* once say!

Chapter One

Making a Choice; the Birth of Spy Fiction

Let me suggest to you a game which, to my mind at least, is the most entertaining and natural way I know to end any dinner party or informal gathering of friends. It's nothing too complex but when the dishes have been cleared away and coffee served it could be just the time to tax the brain a little and drag your guests out of their after-dinner atrophy.

Ask them, over the brandy or the port or whatever you choose to offer for their delectation, to name the three greatest spy writers of the past hundred or so years and then explain the reasons for their choice. Let's see if they match with your already chosen three, perhaps named and written down in a sealed envelope.

You don't have to stick to spy fiction. You might want people to name writers of detective stories. Or possibly poets, science fiction specialists, travel writers, whatever – the list of potentials is endless. But, speaking personally, I have found that the genre of spy writing has always been particularly bountiful in these late evening moments.

There are so many gifted writers to choose from, writers who have spent all their creative lives working in the genre of spy fiction – espionage fiction as they like to call it. On the other hand, there are men and women who have dabbled once or twice with spy stories and then moved on to other things, never to look back or reconsider their options.

Spy novels and spy stories have become increasingly popular over the last hundred and fifty years, so that now books about spying are probably the best-selling volumes of literature to be found in any bookshop. It has been a monumental leap forward for a literary genre that, at the close of the nineteenth century, was a niche market that nobody, not least the writers themselves, really understood.

Arguably this development is a reflection on the state of the world but that should not take away the fact that good spy writing is a genre which has all of the hallmarks we so admire and look for in our escapist literature – courage (albeit often understated), fascinating and multi-layered characters, a struggle to the death between good and bad, and examples of dogged determination in the face of overwhelming odds.

Our concept of 'the spy' has been formed by countless novels and short stories but perhaps even more so by a stream of television and film productions that regularly assail our eyes and ears. It began, of course, with countless B movie features in the 1930s and was followed up by the much-beloved film noir offerings of the 40s and 50s. Nowadays we have multi-million-pound franchises like the Jason Bourne epistles, the *Mission Impossible* movies and the James Bond series of films. When viewed objectively, it seems as if the spy movie has established itself at the top of the tree and is never going to relinquish its position.

Television series like *Spooks* and *The Sandbaggers, Callan* and *The Prisoner*, even a one-off programme like *Vigil*, where the action takes place largely on board a nuclear-powered submarine, have simply added to the appeal. Rarely does a week go by without some espionage-related offering gracing the TV screen.

Yet despite this barrage of visual entertainment, the written word remains dominant and the spy novel is still the main spear carrier for the genre. The range of venues and periods within the over-arching term spy novel is vast, with writers catering for all interests.

Stories have been cleverly crafted around espionage in the Middle Ages, in the Victorian period, even in the future where the dystopian nature of the chosen age gives writers leave to extend their imaginations in all sorts of ways. And the reading public appears to be constantly crying out for more. It would, I think, be fair to say that the two arms of the genre – the written word and the visual interpretation – work seamlessly off each other, constantly building and growing their reputations.

The spy story, like the detective tale, is ideal for adaptation onto the 'silver screen' where, whatever you might think of individual offerings, it has been provided with a realistic visual arm or element. The long list of Bond movies is proof positive of the desire to give that visual representation to the stories – even in the early days of the 007 franchise when success depended on the acting ability of Sean Connery and others, long before the idea of gadgetry took over.

Despite this, however, most of us retain our pre-set, pre-ordained vision of the spy and his world. Once planted in your brain it is difficult to alter or discard the original impression.

Say 'Spy' and the image that flashes into the minds of most people is of the desperate little man working alone at his radio set in a dusty attic or searching frantically for shelter in a darkened wood or across a rugged mountainside. In all cases, the spy is hunted by vastly superior numbers. It has become a seminal image in our imaginations. Indeed, it has become almost a cliché.

Having said that, all clichés have a basis in truth and our interpretation of the lonely spy matched against what appears to be insurmountable odds, is no different from any of the factual accounts that we were fed as children.

Captain Scott facing certain death in Antarctica, General Gordon staring down the Mahdi's hoards in Khartoum armed only with his swagger stick, Colonel Travis and Davy Crockett holed up in the Alamo and so on – the stories are legion. They may not be examples of spying but they are perfect exemplars, each of them in turn, for your imagination to take hold.

So, let's return to the three greatest spy writers of the last hundred years. It might be revealing my preferences and predilections at too early a stage and I could also be very wrong with my choices but I would be amazed if John le Carré did not feature strongly in the lists of most people. Even those who do not regard themselves as followers of spy fiction will know his name and might even have read some of his books.

The other two vacancies or openings are perhaps a little more circumspect and uncertain. Again, many might disagree with the names I have put forward but I'm sure that whoever the nominees might be, they can be argued over indefinitely with points made both for and against whoever is proposed. It's all part of that entertaining after-dinner game!

What makes things somewhat difficult is the simple fact that very often people cannot agree on what spy fiction – indeed, what the profession of spying – is all about.

The dictionary definition of a spy is that he or she is someone who quietly and surreptitiously observes and reports on the work of others. It has to be admitted that spies do actually do this. And yet there is more, much more, to the art of being a spy.

Not only do spies report back on the movement of enemy forces and operations, they also organise opposition to the regime they are spying on. From that position, their role develops from mere reportage into carrying out acts of sabotage and eliminating enemy agents.

Spies invariably work in enemy territory – in, that is, both physical and emotional enemy territory. They are in constant danger and stride the thin line between espionage and counter-espionage. Their work is unglamorous and dangerous, about as far removed from the James Bond image of the elegant, high-living agent as you can possibly get.

For a long while the art of spying was considered a second-rate and degraded occupation and this attitude rubbed off on the reading public when it came to spy stories:

> Spying was regarded as something despicable and no spy could be considered as a hero. Nor was it ever considered desirable that that chief villain of a story should be a spy.

Making a Choice; the Birth of Spy Fiction

> A thief, yes; a murderer, most certainly; but a spy was the nineteenth century equivalent of a sexual pervert.[1]

As we shall see, that was a viewpoint which changed as the nineteenth century drew to a close and the guns of modern warfare became more and more powerful. As stakes grew higher and as Empires increased in size it became imperative that the secret dealings of Britain, France, Russia or Germany should remain secret. At the same time, governments were equally as eager to gain notice, to catch a glimpse of what was going on in the mind of the enemy. Espionage and counter-espionage agents were suddenly elevated to the high table – and spy fiction went along with them.

So, favourite spy writers. No doubt every spy aficionado out there will have his or her favourites. There is nobody to say if they are right or wrong, least of all me, no one to decide whether their loyalty to one writer or another is well-founded or misplaced. I make no judgement and expect to be howled down by readers and critics alike for my own selections. Let me point out that what follows here is a highly personalised choice, *my* highly personalised choice. You, the reader, may agree or disagree as you choose.

Suffice to say that the works of the three writers I have highlighted, The Triumvirate as I have grandly christened them, would grace any library or bookshelf at home, school or college. They are the tip of an ever-growing iceberg, the chief representatives of a genre which has developed and mushroomed in both quality and quantity since the days of the first specialists in the art of spy fiction.

I firmly believe that development, that growth, to be something which could not have happened without my favourite three! But we need to begin by looking back beyond them. People like Baroness Orczy, William Le Queux and Erskine Childers may have preceded them, laying or preparing the ground, just as Len Deighton, Frederick Forsyth and dozens of others have followed in their wake. But no matter who came first or last these three took spy fiction, each in their own way, and moulded it into something quite special.

In the influence they have had on the reading public and on their colleagues who produced and continue to produce high-quality work, I genuinely believe these three to be the most significant writers of Twentieth Century espionage or spy literature.

Of course, it goes beyond that. Forget spy fiction for a moment; in my mind, there is no doubt that they are also a trio of the most popular and influential fiction writers of all time. I want to emphasise that. The Triumvirate took stories of spies and counter-spies out of a narrow, niche market and moved them into the world of fiction writing per se. These three men are, I believe, amongst the leading producers of twentieth century fiction.

My nominated three are John Buchan, Ian Fleming and, as might be expected after my earlier comment, John le Carré. They are all quite different from each other, both in their writing styles and in the nature of their plots and characters. However, the one thing they all own is the ability to weave an atmospheric story and to people it with memorable characters.

Quality writers they may have been but they were not always perfect performers on the printed page, both when they first wrote and now when tastes have changed and when society is a very different beast. There is the distinct possibility that their books might now be regarded by some as being rather unfashionable.

The three writers certainly held views which make them, perhaps, out of date in these more 'enlightened times'. Many might even say that some of those views are objectionable. That does not affect their literary skill. And it does not make them any less exceptional as writers who operated within a genre that, at first glance, might seem limited.

What is beyond doubt is the fact that all three members of The Triumvirate had a unique ability to catch the attention of their readers. More importantly, they were able to hold that interest, usually for years on end.

On a personal level, I invariably read *Greenmantle, From Russia with Love*, and *Tinker, Tailor, Soldier, Spy* at least once every year. Sometimes I substitute *Mr Standfast, Thunderball* or *Smiley's People*. Whichever example I choose, they are all never less than fascinating and each time I read them I find more to enjoy on almost every page.

Other readers, I know, will have a similar fascination, not just with my Triumvirate but with other writers who they consider superior or at the very least equal to my chosen three. Only books of great quality will stand re-reading and scrutiny of such intensity.

All three members of The Triumvirate were seminal exponents of their art. Without them it is doubtful if the genre of spy writing, spy thrillers – call it what you will – would ever have managed to achieve such influence in the literary world. They were, and still are, the standard bearers of popular modern fiction.

What follows here is a tribute to The Triumvirate but it is not a non-stop, unstinting work of praise. As well as stressing their skills, I have attempted to outline their weaknesses, at least as far as I can see them, and put the three writers and their work into the context of the time in which their material was produced.

That is a crucial point for those who consider *Goldfinger, The Thirty-Nine Steps* and *The Spy Who Came in From the Cold* to be outdated.

Quality fiction can never be outdated. Would you call *Great Expectations* outdated? Or *Wuthering Heights*? *Pride and Prejudice* might be considered mannered and irrelevant but it is of its time and is representative of that time. It can never be regarded as being out of its period. It is the same with the work of The Triumvirate.

This brief look at The Triumvirate is a biographical approach but it is not one that stops with just the 'Big Three'. Other writers are discussed, measured against le Carré and his comrades. If your particular favourite is not included, I can only apologise – this is, after all, a personal choice.

One of the aims of this book is to introduce the three writers to people who may not have yet encountered them. If it helps readers go off and explore for themselves the work of Buchan, Fleming and le Carré – and, arguably, some of the other writers who are also mentioned and discussed – then it will have achieved at least part of its objective.

The lives of the writers who make up my Triumvirate are, in themselves, fascinating and well worth studying. All three were what might be termed modern Renaissance men, with skills and interests which stretched a great deal further than their pens and notebooks.

Le Carré was an inveterate traveller and political commentator of some note, being particularly virulent about the recent Brexit policy, about US President Donald Trump and about the USSR's Vladimir Putin. He was so violently opposed to the idea of Britain leaving the European Union that, according to his son, le Carré even applied for Irish citizenship in the months before he died.

Le Carré was, it is alleged, the man who invented two phrases that are central to the modern spy epic – 'the honey trap' and 'moles'. And in between all of that he managed to find time to become a first-class downhill skier.

Ian Fleming was also a sportsman, a renowned performer on the ski slopes of Europe, a low handicap golfer and scuba diver. He was at his happiest in the heat of the Caribbean where he spent half of every year. He loved courting danger, at sea and on the ski slopes, rarely shirking a challenge or an offer to extend his knowledge.

He was also the man who wrote *Chitty-Chitty-Bang-Bang,* one of the most memorable children's books of his age. He loved to gamble and was particularly good at it. In 2008 the Times voted him 14th in its list of great British writers from the post-Second World War years.

John Buchan, a skilled climber and mountaineer, even went on record as saying that he regarded himself as a politician first, a writer second! For a writer of his stature and reputation, that is no mean statement.

Making a Choice; the Birth of Spy Fiction

Buchan was a Member of Parliament who served the government and the country in a wide range of roles. At the end of his life, he became a renowned and well-loved diplomat. And despite all that, he managed to write over 100 books, everything from fiction and poetry to history and biography – not bad for a man who claimed that writing was only his second-best skill!

All three had been involved in the business of spying, at one level or another, either before or during their time as writers of spy fiction. Fleming and le Carré were ground-level operatives while Buchan, already schooled and educated in the mayhem of government double-dealing, rose to giddy and dazzling heights in the Propaganda Department during the First World War.

The old adage of 'writing about what you know' certainly helped the members of The Triumvirate to achieve in their chosen field – indeed, out of all the 'top' spy writers who came to prominence before, during and after the Second World War only one had no direct involvement in the art of espionage. That was Eric Ambler and he, like almost all of his books, was always a little different from the mainstream.

All three members of The Triumvirate retained an intense interest in and knowledge of their subject, revelling in its minuscule cracks and complications. An understanding of their lives, of what they did and why they did it, can only help to increase enjoyment of their work. Good luck with what you may find.

Let me, for a minute, drop into self-indulgence and finish this prelude – if that is what it is – by being as effete and contrived as any of the early spy writers who pre-dated my Triumvirate.

In all humility, I offer you these few words of advice, something that might guide you as you make a footfall, tentative or otherwise, into this book. The words are not mine but I sincerely wish they were. They come from the Triumvirate.

As any of Fleming's memorable villains might have said 'Welcome, Mr Bond, I have been expecting you.' Without being too presumptuous, it is a warm welcome, not something that the Bond villains intended but real nonetheless.

In the words of Richard Hannay's friend and mentor Sandy Arbuthnot may you find herein 'a list of the Twelve Major Virtues and the Ninety-Nine Names of God' – your own version of course.

And, perhaps inevitably, as Toby Esterhase once told George Smiley 'Take care, George. Go well, hear me?' It's simple but exceedingly good advice. No more prevarication, read the book.

***

While Britain can undoubtedly claim the largest number of writers to have specialised in writing spy fiction, credit for the first spy story must lie elsewhere. Despite the morality or, rather, lack of morality involved in the spying profession, the origins of spy literature have a distinctly religious flavour.

To be precise, the world's first spy stories come from the Bible. Let's start with the Book of Joshua. Spies sent by General Joshua into the city of Jericho not only manage to bring back vital information about the city defences but also succeed in 'turning' Rachal the Harlot. Elegantly done, that 'turning' of enemy agents is something which spies and counter spies from all sides have been attempting to achieve ever since.

Also in the Old Testament, in the Book of Numbers, we learn that the patriarch Moses sent twelve spies into Canaan. The number is important containing, as it does, one representative from each of the twelve tribes of Israel. The spies were to assess the strength of opposition in the country and the readiness of the various citadels to face attack. Unfortunately, they returned with false information which resulted in the children of Israel wandering in the desert for many years.

China played a pivotal role in the early development of the spy tale. Not a piece of fiction but still enormously readable, *Ping Fa* came into being in 510 BC. The world's first textbook on spying, it was a work so accurate and so useful that it was reprinted in English and issued to British forces in North Africa during the Second World War.

In the late thirteenth century, Lo Kuan-chung produced *The Romance of the Three Kingdoms* but this was a book of factual recollections and cannot therefore be regarded as a work of spy fiction. As a 'textbook' about spying, however, it cannot be faulted.

Until late in the fifteenth century storytelling had always been an oral art form and in Europe – the Celtic nations in particular – travelling bards would regularly call at the palaces of the great and good in order to spin their tales. The trouble with oral storytelling is that it was then and remains now a transitory art form. Unless someone took the trouble to write down the tales as they were spoken, once delivered to the audience the only record of the story lay in the memories of those who listened.

Things began to change with the arrival of the printing press. In the late 1450s, over one hundred years after the world's first mass-produced book – Wang Chen's *Nung Shu*, a treatise on agriculture and farming – Johannes Gutenberg developed a printing press in Germany. It revolutionised the world of literature and reading and under the influence of Thomas Caxton and Wynkyn da Worde its use quickly spread to the British Isles.

Despite the new printing process, the novel in Britain was slow to develop. It was late in the eighteenth century before Samuel Richardson's *Pamela* and Henry Fielding's double whammy of *Joseph Andrews* and *Tom Jones* hit the bookshops, causing an explosion of interest from the public that has never yet gone away. Despite that sudden interest, apart from one notable exception, the spy novel had to wait even longer before it came rearing and plunging onto the bookshelves.

That exception was the product of American writer James Fenimore Cooper. To him must go the accolade of being the first spy novelist when in 1821 he wrote and published *The Spy*. It was Fenimore

Cooper's initial venture into the business of writing and was hugely successful. But the theme of spying was an isolated occurrence as the young writer soon turned away from the genre and went on to produce more renowned books like *The Last of the Mohicans* and other tales of the American frontier.

Set in North America during the War of Independence, *The Spy* is more the story of accidental adventure than it is a record of espionage daring-do. The plot line concerns Harvey Birch, a British army officer who attempts to visit relatives living behind the American lines in New England. Captured by the rebel forces he is accused of spying and is sentenced to death. The story then centres on Birch's escape and his journey back to safety. It is not really a spy story in the way we know and love our spy stories today but at least it was an acknowledgement of the value and dangers of spying in wartime.

Fenimore Cooper returned to the spy genre ten years after *The Spy* when he published *The Bravo*, a story based around the duplicity of nation-states like Venice. This book was more like modern spy stories, relying for its effect on the Machiavellian attitudes and schemes of governments while they are hiding behind the veneer of good nature and bonhomie.

After Fenimore Cooper's two efforts, however, the spy novel went into some form of self-induced hibernation and had to wait for a considerable period of time before being dusted off and resurrected.

Detective fiction was the precursor of espionage tales, writers like Charles Dickens and Wilkie Collins lending their considerable weight to the genre with books like *Our Mutual Friend*, *The Woman in White* and *The Moonstone*. Dickens's untimely death undoubtedly cut short further development in this line and, surmise as it might be, in all probability the great master himself may have launched into spy fiction. As it was, we were left with just a few hints and possibilities in his intriguingly unfinished final book, *The Mystery of Edwin Drood*.

Detective fiction, like spy stories, depends on the drawing power of the central character, usually the detective himself. That is one of the reasons why the Sherlock Holmes stories of Arthur Conan Doyle have remained so popular with the reading public. Doyle took Holmes into the realms of spy fiction on only two separate occasions – *The Bruce Partington Plans* and *His Last Bow.* The stories are not Conan Doyle's greatest work but they do reflect the overwhelming public interest in betrayal and the fear of British secrets landing up in enemy hands.

The end of the nineteenth century was the age of Empire, a time when British, French and German Imperialism was at its height. As a result, stories from this era tended to centre on the rivalry between European powers and the drive for dominance, particularly in Asia, by nations with dreams of colonial power. Exotic locations were an essential element in the makeup of such stories.

In particular, the romance of the North-West Frontier where Russia was supposedly flexing its muscles ready to wrest control of the Indian sub-continent away from Britain had great appeal to both readers and writers. It was a world that most readers – and many of the writers – would never visit or experience. Consequently, accuracy was not high on the list of attributes of these early spy writers and readers.

Rudyard Kipling, however, had been born and lived in India. He was quick to produce a book that many now believe to be the original spy novel, the fountainhead from which all subsequent espionage tales developed and spread. *Kim* first saw the light of day as a serial in McClure's Magazine in 1901 and then in novel form later the same year. It was a seriously good piece of fiction, redolent with atmosphere and adventure and can justifiably be regarded as Kipling's finest work.

The book tells the story of orphan Kim and his travels along the rugged borders of India where he meets many memorable characters. Kim, of course, is a child – however precocious he might be – and he is little more than a malleable implement in the hands of his controller Mahbut Ali and the British secret service.

The orphan Kim was certainly not a spy in the way we have come to expect our representatives of the secret world. It hardly mattered. The reading public took to the book, revelling in its exotic detail, its scents and smells that forced them, metaphorically at least, out of their comfy armchairs and into the Indian sub-continent.

In particular, the public heeded the warning that the borders of their Empire were under threat and that therefore there was a need to monitor Russian activity on the North-West Frontier of Afghanistan and India. That was the country for 'young men', Kipling and his like seemed to be saying, and that was where spying and watching the Russians quickly became known as 'The Great Game'. Even the Music Halls of London and other great cities embraced the moment with dramatic monologues like *The Green Eye of the Little Yellow God* and Kipling's *Road to Mandalay* becoming firm favourites.

The first real advance in spy fiction, however, came a few years after *Kim*. It came in the shape of Baroness Emma Orczy, a disenfranchised Hungarian novelist who was then living in Britain.

Her great hero was the foppish and romantic Sir Percy Blakeney, the Scarlet Pimpernel as he has become known, a man who spent years rescuing French aristocrats from 'Madame Guillotine' during the Napoleonic Wars. Unlike her predecessors, Baroness Orczy's hero had nothing to do with India, the Far East or the North West Frontier.

Beginning with a stage play in 1903, Orczy produced twelve Scarlet Pimpernel stories between 1905 and 1940, the character having several close shaves but only once being apprehended by the French authorities – who failed to recognise him and let him go! Hugely popular, the stories caught the imagination of the public and even saw London urchins chanting the famous rhyme or poem from one of her books extolling the success of the character:

> They seek him here, they seek him there,
> Those Frenchies seek him everywhere.
> Is he in Heaven, is he in Hell,
> That damned elusive Pimpernel.[2]

Hardly a spy, nevertheless Sir Percy worked undercover with a false identity that was so effective it was not really challenged by the authorities. Never a government employee, in Orczy's books Blakeney acted solely on his own initiative. The series later sparked several Hollywood films and even modern versions such as *Pimpernel Smith* where the eponymous hero is brought up to date and is found to be fighting against Nazi Germany.

During the apogee of the Scarlet Pimpernel, another writer emerged into prominence. This was William Tufnell Le Queux. A strange man, someone who had enormous difficulty separating fact from fiction, Le Queux specialised in what became known as Invasion Literature.

The genre of Invasion Literature was hugely popular in the first decade of the twentieth century when fear of the growing German military and naval strength was rampant in both Britain and France. Britain, in particular, was wary of the Kaiser's massive fleet of dreadnought battleships and Le Queux and other lesser figures used fiction to forewarn the people and the government of what would happen to the country if drastic steps were not taken.

Hugely popular, with his books selling in their thousands, Le Queux quickly became a prophet of doom, so much so that in 1909 a sub-section of the Committee of Imperial Defence was called in order to discuss and find an answer to the vast amount of espionage that Le Queux and, it seemed, the entire British public believed was going on in the country. William Le Queux was one of those called to give evidence to the committee.

Out of the sub-committee emerged the official British secret service and, of course, William Le Queux sold even more books. *The Invasion of 1910* marked the high-water level of his output but he continued with his sensationalist stories such as *Spies of the Kaiser* until the outbreak of the First World War. By then Le Queux had been rather overtaken by better writers and more deliberate or explicit spy novelists.

The first decade of the twentieth century saw many writers, well respected and admired in other literary genres, turn their hands to the writing of spy books. Notable amongst these was Joseph Conrad whose 1907 novel *The Secret Agent* was a complicated mixture of a dramatic adventure story and a study of marginalised individuals in society.

Amongst other well-known writers who tried their hand at spy fiction in these years before the First World War were Saki (Hugh Monroe) and E Phillips Oppenheim. The British public lapped up their offerings, even Queen Alexandria, wife of the British king, became a fan of such literature.

One of the most prolific and most popular spy/adventure writers for both children and adults in this period was Max, later Sir Max, Pemberton. Editor of magazines like *Chums* and *The Cassell's Magazine*, he was a friend of Arthur Conan Doyle and William Le Queux. His best sellers included *The Iron Pirate,* featuring a gas-driven ironclad warship and, more specifically, the spy-orientated *Kronstadt* which came out to huge acclaim in1898.

In the closing years of the nineteenth century, interest in spying had been given further impetus by the Dreyfus Affair, a long-running scandal involving the wrongful imprisonment of a French artillery officer who was charged with and convicted of selling information and state secrets to the Germans. Accusations of treason and betrayal were thrown about like confetti, along with a strong strain of anti-Semitism before Alfred Dreyfus was exonerated in 1906, declared innocent and released from Devil's Island.

What made the Dreyfus Affair such a potent factor was the simple fact that it was real. This was no piece of fiction from the pens of men like William Le Queux or Joseph Conrad, it was actual fact with shady dealings and wrongful arrest. It might have happened in

France but everybody knew that it could just as easily have occurred in Britain or in any part of her vast Empire.

Events in France were one thing but the book which took spy fiction to a new level was *The Riddle of the Sands*. A revolutionary offering, it was written by Erskine Childers, Irish adventurer and future martyr to the cause of Irish independence. His book was published to great acclaim in 1903, taking reality to new heights and causing a furore of interest in the public.

The Riddle of the Sands was a fast-moving action adventure involving two friends sailing around the Frisian Islands and coastal waters of North Germany. It was based on yachting trips that Childers himself had made, giving the background to the story an edge of realism that was missing in the work of Le Queux and others.

However, it was in the mass of detail, all verifiable and honest, contained in the book that made *Riddle of the Sands* so special. The Admiralty quickly realised from Childers' story that their charts of the area were inadequate and out of date and, with war looming over the horizon, that was a problem needing to be dealt with. They immediately sent out a survey team to the Frisian area in order to rectify the situation.

In many respects, the storyline and basic premise of *The Riddle of the Sands* are no different from many of the other examples of Invasion Literature. An invasion of Britain is planned by the villainous German Kaiser but is thwarted at the last moment by intrepid defenders of the nation – seemingly standard stuff in the genre of Invasion Literature.

In Childers's book, the senior officers of the German Navy have concocted an ingenious and unexpected invasion scheme involving dozens of flat-bottomed barges full of Prussian soldiers being towed across the North Sea by vessels from the High Seas Fleet. The intention is to land the invasion force on the isolated and virtually undefended area of East Anglia north of the Thames. The Kaiser even arrives on the scene to inspect what he is convinced will be the means of Britain's downfall.

In that overall aim, and certainly at first glance, the book might appear to be similar to many other works of Invasion Literature, but in actual fact, *The Riddle of the Sands* is about as far removed from the mass of invasion scare material as the dark side of the moon.

Above all, it is immensely readable, something that so many offerings in the genre are not! However, it is also the realism and the detail of the writing which make Childers' story stand out as being a class above the run-of-the-mill invasion tales.

Childers probably did not realise the effect his technique would have but he filled his pages with facts and details, information that was chilling in its accuracy, compelling in its insistence. This attention to detail was a new departure for escapist literature and made his book something special. It certainly set it apart from the standard invasion scare stories.

The Riddle of the Sands was, to put it simply, a groundbreaking work of art. And that is something which is often forgotten in the welter of accolades with which it has been saddled. It is now, over a hundred years since it was first published, almost universally accepted that the book is one of the earliest and most effective pieces of espionage writing.

Quite apart from terrifying the British public and government, attention to minute detail was a new technique that was a revelation to the readers of spy and invasion literature. It was also later used by, of all people, the great Triumvirate of Ian Fleming, John Buchan and John Le Carré!

Almost every Bond story begins with 007 being briefed by a specialist who offers in-depth background information that will prove essential to Bond's mission. At some length he is lectured on subjects as diverse as gold, rocket science, diamonds and whatever issue is central to the storyline.

In *Goldfinger*, the flippant Bond is even presented with a bar of gold – along with the sage advice from M that it is to be returned to the Royal Mint once he has used it to catch the eye and the greed of Mr Goldfinger!

Buchan uses a similar trick in his Richard Hannay books with the intrepid hero being intensively briefed by Sir Walter Bullivant or, in *The Thirty-Nine Steps*, by burying his nose in material such as Scudder's little black notebook.

Buchan artfully keeps the reader's interest alive by having Hannay fail – at first glance – to unravel Scudder's code. Everyone knows that our hero will, sooner or later, go back to discover the key to the mystery.

George Smiley is the arch researcher who in books like *Tinker, Tailor, Soldier, Spy* even moves into a run-down and undistinguished little hotel in Paddington where he can delve deeply into the problem he has been set without fear of interruption.

Smiley's quest for the mole or traitor lodged within the British Secret Service is really an academic exercise, involving Smiley trawling through masses of secret documents and long-forgotten files. The action, such as it is, occurs only in the final phase of the book.

Like the later Triumvirate, Erskine Childers eagerly seized on similar attention to detail – something which other writers of Invasion Literature of the time shunned as unnecessary waffle. Such detail would, they felt, be of no interest to the readers.

And yet Childers took it, used it, made a virtue out of it. In fact, the audience for Childers' book thoroughly enjoyed the detail, feeling that they were there with Carruthers and Davies on the mud flats of North Germany:

> Good heavens! What was that? I stopped short and listened. From over the water on my left there rang out, dulled by fog but distinct to the ear, three double strokes of a bell or gong. I looked at my watch.
>
> "Ship at anchor," I said to myself. "Six bells in the afternoon watch." I knew the Balje was here, a deep roadstead where a vessel entering the Eastern Ems might well anchor to ride out a fog.

> I was just stepping forward when another sound followed from the same quarter, a bugle-call this time. Then I understood – only men-of-war sound bugles – the *Blitz* was here then; and very natural, too, I thought, and strode on.
>
> The sand was growing drier, the water further beneath me; then came a thin black ribbon of weed – the high-water mark. A few cautious steps to the right and I touched tufts of marram grass.³

And so on, the detail impressing itself on the authenticity of the writing. Far from boring the reader Childers' attention to tiny details such as in the example quoted above – and there are many more – is what makes the book significant and a lasting contribution to spy literature.

As the world lurched closer and ever closer to a catastrophic war, interest in spying and in spy fiction showed no sign of abating. Facing up to the enemy on the battlefield was one thing, having him undermine your efforts back home was entirely different and spy thrillers tapped into what was a compelling mixture of fear, excitement and satisfaction.

Fear of fifth columnists simply grew and the pulp fiction writers like Le Queux made themselves a fortune on the proceeds. Even Joseph Conrad produced another spy novel, *Under Western Skies*, a complex and difficult work that left most of the admirers of pulp fiction trailing in its wake.

The fictional world of espionage was jolted by reality in the final years of peace. Two supposed anarchist outrages in London, incidents which were in fact the result of botched jewellery robberies and which had nothing to do with the anarchist ideals of the time, helped fuel what appeared to be an insatiable desire for spy and counter-spy novels.

The two outrages, the robbery aspects of which were conveniently shelved or ignored in favour of arson and murder by anarchists, caused a frisson of fear and panic. It was a delicious sense of horror that easily fed the fictional world of the early spy novelists.

In the minds of the general public – bolstered by an increasingly rampant and vitriolic press – anarchists were just one step removed from German secret agents in their desire to cause harm to the British Empire. And the two outrages served simply to further fuel the emotion.

The Tottenham Outrage of 1909 took place after a failed robbery by a collection of immigrant refugees. It concluded with over 400 pistol shots being fired wildly into the air and involved a chase across North London with fugitives and the pursuing policemen riding on, of all things, a number of lumbering tramcars.

This faintly ludicrous element was offset by the tragedy of twenty-three casualties, including a policeman and a ten-year-old boy who were both shot and killed. The origin of the shots – from police or robbers – was unknown.

The unfolding drama was watched by thousands, who clustered on the pavements and peered from the windows of the houses that lined the route of the chase. This was excitement and real-life drama occurring under their very noses.

After several hours of chases and gun battles, the surviving robbers, finally realising that escape was now impossible, committed suicide. In their wake, they left the British public with a wild sense of betrayal and anger that their hospitality in allowing the immigrants to set up home in London had been violently abused.

The more famous Siege of Sydney Street was an altogether more serious matter. It occurred in January 1910 and was a curious affair, badly handled by the authorities but with enough violence and threat to convince the British public that an anarchist uprising was on the cards:

> Two Latvian refugees, after killing three unarmed policemen during a bungled robbery, were besieged in an

East London lodging house, surrounded by units of the British army. Winston Churchill, then Home Secretary, arrived to watch proceedings which concluded with the house on fire and the suicide of the two Latvians.[4]

Churchill, himself a reader of Invasion Literature, would have liked nothing more than to charge at the head of the besieging soldiers into the Latvian's lodging house. He was prevented from doing so by his closest advisors, probably just as well as the future Prime Minister and saviour of the country would undoubtedly have found himself fatally shot or wounded. Even so, despite all the advice Churchill still managed to get himself photographed at the front of attacking soldiers, unable to keep out of the action and the limelight!

The siege lasted for several hours, newspaper headline writers revelling in the story. The Latvian's shelter was eventually riddled by bullets, even by artillery shellfire, and was set on fire before finally being stormed by police and the army. Two of the Latvian refugees, the only ones found in the house, died, either by self-inflicted gunshot wounds or from the attacking police and soldiers.

If events such as the Tottenham Outrage and the Siege of Sydney Street could occur in real life, right under the noses of the police and government, then as far as the public was concerned the cosy world of the British Empire was under direct threat. Dead policemen and children did not bear too close scrutiny.

Retreat into the fictional world – that at least was safe! The future of spy/anarchist/ revolutionary literature was suddenly well assured. On the printed page the words and deeds of anarchists or enemy spies could not hurt you and one thing was clear above everything else – good would inevitably triumph in the end.

The only thing now was to ensure that the genre emerged from the grasping hands of the pulp writers like William Le Queux to become the literary property of quality authors. For that to happen it needed those 'quality authors' to be available – and more importantly, to be willing to put their reputations on the line. Enter John Buchan.

Chapter Two

John Buchan, a Child of the Kirk

John Buchan was a lowland Scot, born in the town of Perth on the banks of the river Tay on 26 August 1875. His father, also called John, was a Minister of the Free Church of Scotland and at the time of his eldest son's birth, the Reverend Buchan was the controlling factor in Knox Kirk in the bustling town.

The Knox Kirk was a temporary appointment, which was probably just as well. The Reverend Buchan's seventeen-year-old wife Helen was finding it difficult to cope with the pressure of running a home and dealing with the demands of a new baby.

The pressures of the parish were bearing down heavily on the recently married couple and money was short. What was needed was a new opportunity and a new position, Rev Buchan's time at Knox Kirk having been a poor enough start for the young clergyman's career. And indeed, things soon began to change.

Within a year the Reverend Buchan was 'called' to a new, permanent parish at Pathhead on the coast of Fife. The manse which came with the job offered a welcome home for the growing family. The house stood on the side of a hill above the harbour of Kirkaldy close to a large linoleum factory, the town railway line and a blacking works. There the Reverend Buchan and his family were assailed by the noise and smell of industrial Scotland.

John Buchan and his siblings, particularly his brother Willie, loved it. The hurly-burly of the time and the small-boy gang warfare around the docks, endemic to almost all industrial locations, was perfect for the development of the Buchan children. John soon grew to be the leader in many of the mad-cap escapades of his 'gang':

It was JB who led them into the most mischief – for example, setting light to tar barrels and rolling them into a disused quarry. After a particularly egregious misdemeanour the local policeman, who was an Elder of the Free Church, remarked that "I'll hae to jail thae bairns and leave the Kirk."[1]

The policeman was spared the indignity of having to leave his church but it was more by accident than design. When he was just five years old John Buchan fell from a horse-drawn carriage in which he was travelling. The carriage wheels passed over his head, knocking him unconscious and rendering him close to death. An operation relieved the pressure on his brain but for almost twelve months Buchan lay in his bed, swathed in bandages and with orders not to move.

It could have been a disastrous time for the energetic boy but, instead, what the enforced inactivity did was simply to free up his imagination and together with his wild – although temporarily dormant – sense of freedom create the mind which, when he was ready, would produce some of the greatest adventure stories of the age.

During his year-long period of enforced idleness, the young Buchan lay in bed, not allowed to take exercise or even read. But nothing could stop that fertile imagination taking root and transporting him to lands and wild regions far away from his native home. He was allowed to talk, with his parents and siblings, and he became an engaging conversationalist, a talent that was to remain with him all his life.

To use a good old-fashioned cliché, there is no such thing as a bad experience. Such inactivity was hardly what Buchan would have chosen for himself but it was invaluable training and preparation for the man and the writer he would grow to be.

Luckily there was no lasting damage from the injury and after twelve months he was up and about again, his head still wrapped in bandages. The only permanent damage was a large swelling on the left side of his face. It hardly worried the newly released young Buchan who quickly resumed his wild ways. He roamed the streets of the town, revelling in the sights and smells and talking to sailors who regaled him with stories about their travels and the far-off places that were so appealing to the young boy's imagination.

The difference now was that he was allowed to read again and the works of Sir Walter Scott and Robert Louis Stevenson soon became his favourite reading matter. In particular, the romance and adventure of Scott's world became his habitual retreat, a world that was alive and breathing in his head. Scott and Stevenson, like Buchan, had spent long, enforced periods in bed as children and like their new acolyte, they had used the time effectively.

The other great influence and appeal to Buchan, then and throughout his life, was John Bunyan and his book *Pilgrim's Progress*. This seventeenth-century Puritan offering implanted itself in the young man's brain and remained there throughout all the trials and tribulations that lay ahead. He had been encouraged to read Bunyan's Christian allegory by his parents but once he started on the text Buchan did not need much encouragement to keep reading and to make the book a life-long passion. He was later to use the work effectively, as part of a secret code, in his third Richard Hannay spy book *Mr Standfast*.

Buchan's first taste of formal education was short-lived, taking place at the small Dame School close to his home. He was expelled when his wild temperament saw him cause damage to the teacher's property – actually he kicked over a saucepan of soup boiling on the fire! Next came the Board School in the centre of Kirkaldy. He did well, the two or three-mile walk to and from school each day probably exhausting much of his pent-up energy. He enjoyed the school and was happy there, being placed in the top position in his class.

He was ferociously Scottish, his intense reading of Scott and Stevenson advancing his nationalism. He was well versed in his country's history and took immense pride in Scottish victories on the battlefield, particularly against their English neighbours. By his own account, he felt sorry for anyone who was not Scottish!

Summer holidays with his extended family in Peebles and Broughton on the Borders gave Buchan the opportunity to live out some of his fantasies, charging through the heather imagining that the redcoats of King George and 'Butcher' Cumberland were hot on his heels. It was 'education' in the purest sense, learning that became a valuable commodity when he was later to send his hero Richard Hannay fleeing for his life across the same hillsides.

When he was not playing out or inventing stories for himself and his siblings, the young Buchan roamed the hillsides and learned to fish in the streams and burns that fed into the River Tweed. He was surprisingly adept at finding, then catching trout. Fishing, like hill walking and rock climbing, became a life-long passion.

***

In November 1888 the Reverend Buchan and his family moved from Pathhead when the still-ambitious Minister was called to a new parish in the Gorbals area of Glasgow. The new church, the John Knox Kirk as it was known, was situated in the middle of the rough, tough working-class area of the city although the Buchans lived two miles away in the more genteel and elegant suburb of Crosshill. John Buchan would be forced, yet again, to walk to school:

> John's daily walk to Hutcheson's Grammar School, and later to Glasgow University, took him past tenements, warehouses, factories, an epitome of industrial Scotland. The other, pastoral, Scotland was for the holidays.[2]

Holidays in the Border country continued to be vitally important for the would-be novelist and his family, particularly the long summer days of August when the world stretched out ahead of them, seemingly running on forever. John, his brothers and sisters, regarded the Borders as home, the area and part of Scotland where they truly belonged.

He did not yet know it but the Upper Tweed and the high hills of Tweedsmuir were crucial in his emotional and literary development. By the time he had reached late adolescence John Buchan could realistically claim to have swum in every pool, climbed every hill and fished in every burn in the area. He made friends with the sheepherders and poachers, farmers and gamekeepers of the region, finding himself at home with all of them, each in their own way.

Back in the Gorbals, the Reverend Buchan was committed to bringing the working men and women of the community to God. Sundays were given to the Kirk but otherwise the elder Buchan was a man who loved – and encouraged his children to love – poetry and verse. Mrs Helen Buchan, on the other hand, had no time for such fripperies. She had grown into a practical and hard-headed woman and would have been highly delighted if her eldest child had decided to make a career in the church. Nothing could have been further from the young man's mind.

The young John Buchan loved learning – but learning for its own sake, not to pass exams or give him qualifications. He saw little purpose in studying simply to gain recognition and, as a consequence, read only what he wanted to read, memorising only the poems and texts that appealed to him. In addition to Sir Walter Scott and Stevenson, these now included poetry by Wordsworth and Milton, prose from writers like Bacon, Hazlitt and Lamb.

Then, in his final year at Hutcheson's, Buchan came under the influence of the school's remarkable Classics teacher, James Cadell, and everything changed. His outlook on life broadened and although he retained his love of 'old favourites', the world of wider literature began to filter into his imagination. In particular, through Cadell's teaching Buchan came to love Latin and Greek.

Later, as an 'old boy' of the school he wrote an article for the school magazine, outlining the effect that the engaging Cadell had on him and his classmates:

> The classics were to him the "humanities" in the broadest sense, and he managed to indoctrinate his pupils with their intrinsic greatness and their profound significance for the modern world.[3]

So profound was the teaching and mentorship of James Cadell that Buchan won a bursary, worth £30 a year, to support him at Glasgow University. It was 1892, he was just sixteen years old and nobody was more amazed at his success than Buchan himself. Self-doubt was a temporary emotion, however, and soon Buchan was relishing his achievements.

At Glasgow University Buchan came under the influence of another great teacher, Gilbert Murray who had been given the Chair of Greek at the University when he was just twenty-three years old. Murray took Buchan under his wing, calling him 'a treasure of a pupil' and encouraging him to try – successfully as it turned out – for a scholarship to Oxford. For the first time, Buchan also began to believe that he might have something of a future as a writer.

In the summer of 1894, he began to keep a commonplace book, a notebook in which he recorded lists of books to read, places to visit and, importantly, books he was planning to write.

The drawing up of lists became a regular occurrence for Buchan. This first one was a doggedly determined outline of what he was intending to do with his life, something which drew criticism from those who saw him as too forthright and too dedicated to achieving success.

In the last years of the 'professional amateur', such criticism may have been justified but young Buchan did not care. He knew where he was going and knew exactly what he had to do.

It was not all ambition and adolescent dreams, far from it. In his first year at Glasgow University, he had already begun to edit an edition of Bacon's essays, complete with an Introduction by himself. He had a publisher lined up – the Walter Scott Publishing Company – and the book duly appeared on the bookstalls in 1894. His first novel, *Sir Quixote of the Moors*, came out a year later.

Buchan's first novel was a piece of historical fiction, centring on a massacre of the Covenanters and a romantic love story set in the remote Scottish hills. It drew heavily on the bleak Scottish landscapes that he had come to know so well during his childhood and adolescence. He was well aware of the power of place in this, his first book. It was a power that he was able to use time and time again in all of his fiction:

> As a child I must have differed in other things besides sanctity from the good Bernard of Clairvaux who, we are told, could walk all day by the Lake of Geneva and never see the lake. My earliest recollections are not of myself, but of my environment. It is only reflection that fits my small presence into the picture.[4]

Sense of place remained a crucial element in all of Buchan's books, particularly the novels. Into the brilliantly constructed descriptions of the environments which hold and contain his characters, he repeatedly pitches his heroes and their opponents, throwing them into conflict not only with each other but also with the hills and forests, the mountains and the rivers that meant so much to him when growing up. It is brilliantly done, the fictional descriptions leaning heavily on the reality of his own experiences, experiences of both the recent and the distant past.

Yet Buchan's work was not all about sense of place. Had it been he would probably have become an early travel writer! John Buchan had much more in mind.

He had an automatic appreciation of people, knowing that the interaction between characters and the environment – a vital melding of people and place– were essential components in the creation of the third 'p' which was then, and remains now, so vital in the production of good fiction – problem. And he was not above using his own family, his own experiences, to make this effective.

The Buchans suffered a family tragedy in 1893 when the youngest daughter Violet died from tuberculosis. It was a crippling fatality for all of the family, particularly for John who had been close to his young sister. The one consolation for all of them, however, was in their religion and their clear belief in life in the hereafter. John, however, had an additional consolation.

As with everything he saw and experienced the young writer stored away the memory of his sister's illness and death and was able to use it in one of his final books *Sick Heart River* where he recounts the final illness and death from TB of his hero Sir Edward Leithen. Leithen's death is all the more poignant and effective because, recollected 'in tranquillity', it was written many years after Violet's passing.

Even at this early stage, Buchan was nothing if not prolific. Within five years of his notebook entry, all three projected or proposed novels, along with a volume of essays and a book of verse about fishing, had been written and published. He was told by many people that his production of so much work would not last. He admitted that he was prolific. Many would have said driven.

***

By the time John Buchan took up his place at Brasenose College, Oxford, in October 1895 he was a year older than most of his contemporaries, was in receipt of a more than useful scholarship and was earning regular sums of money for articles and reviews in renowned and accepted periodicals like *MacMillan's* and

The Gentleman's Magazine. All of this should have made his transition from Glasgow to the gentility of the Home Counties reasonably easy.

However, Buchan's earliest impressions of Oxford were not exactly favourable. Later, in *Memory Hold the Door*, his autobiography written just prior to his death, he was able to analyse the reasons for this lacklustre start to the university that soon became central to his life:

> The soft autumn air did not suit my health; the lectures which I attended seemed jejune and platitudinous, and the regime slack, after the strenuous life of Glasgow; I played no game well enough to acquire an absorbing interest in it. Above all, being a year older than my contemporaries, I felt that I had been pitchforked into a kindergarten. The revels of alcoholic children offended me, and having an unfortunate gift of plain speech, I did not make myself popular ... I must have been at that time an intolerable prig.[5]

In that last sentence Buchan hit on the cause of his initial unhappiness. He had come from a world where he was the centre of all things – popular, admired, loved even – and found himself in an environment where he had to work for acceptance. That was far from easy for a young man who had always seemed able to control all that life threw at him.

Buchan was lucky, however. Brasenose was a small college, situated in the centre of town, and after a while 'out in the cold', he found that was able to make friends easily, both within the confines of his college and in the wider university. Soon his list of friends and acquaintances included men like Hilaire Belloc, Leo Amery and, particularly important, his later business partner the publisher and Oxford rugby captain T A (Tommy) Nelson.

Achievement came naturally to Buchan and, after his rather rocky start, his time at Oxford was one of success followed by further success. To his colleagues and friends, his successes seemed to come easily – in fact, he worked hard at his books and was not ashamed to say so.

In 1898 he won the Newdigate Prize for a poem on the Pilgrim Fathers, having already claimed the Stanhope History Prize the year before. He eventually became President of the Oxford Union. His ambitions were not rooted solely in Oxford, however. In his final year at college, the publisher John Lane accepted a series of essays on Border life and then asked him to become Literary Advisor to the firm. One of the first books he advised Lane to publish was *The Man from the North* by Arnold Bennet.

With the publication of his own second novel, *John Burnet of Barns*, John Buchan was included in the 1898 edition of *Who's Who* – a memorable accomplishment for a young man of just twenty-three who had not yet graduated from his university.

He continued to write for literary magazines, notably *The Yellow Book*, the leading aesthetic and literary magazine of the '90s where he was featured alongside artists like Beardsley, novelists like HG Wells and poets such as W B Yeats.

Many years later the poet John Betjeman was to take a sideways dig at Buchan when he had Oscar Wilde sneer at him in his poem 'The Arrest of Oscar Wile at the Cadogan Hotel'. In Betjeman's 1937 poem Wilde dismissed *The Yellow Book* by declaring 'And Buchan has got in it now'. It was a typical example of the way John Buchan was appreciated at the time – too forward for his own good! The young Scot ploughed on, regardless.

After four years at Oxford, Buchan was awarded a First in Greats, (ancient history, philosophy and the classics) and was considering either a fellowship or possibly even a Chair at Edinburgh University. In the end, however, he decided that he had had enough of academe. He had published five books, including his first non-fiction work, an account of the lives and careers of Scholar Gypsies. Now London and a career 'at the bar' beckoned.

London was a far more expensive place to live than Oxford but Buchan had planned exactly how he would support himself whilst working for his Bar exams. He would write, in books and for magazines and, as if to underline the point, he drew up yet another list of future activities!

In London he became friendly with Leo Strachey and, almost as soon as he arrived in the city, began producing a regular stream of reviews and articles for Strachey's magazine the *Spectator*. The magazine paid well and, more importantly, provided much-needed publicity for the young writer and journalist.

Over the next few months, he became something of a 'man about town,' regularly holding and attending dinner parties and heading off for long weekends in the country. At these meetings, he formed friendships with many important and influential people, men like the Conservative leader Arthur Balfour.

At one crucially important weekend gathering in March 1901, Buchan renewed his acquaintance with his Oxford friend Leo Amery. It was to be a far more important meeting than Buchan could ever have imagined.

Amery had just returned from South Africa where the war against the Boers was then drawing to a close. Lord Alfred Milner, High Commissioner for South Africa, was also back in Britain searching for staff to help with the reconstruction of the Transvaal and the Orange River State, both of them former Boer Republics and now British Colonies. In particular, he was looking for a number of personal assistants or secretaries, men of initiative who could take direction but also had the ability to act on their own instincts.

Following their meeting and renewal of friendship, Amery suggested to Lord Milner that John Buchan would be a suitable candidate. He was young, fit and active, with no family ties – in fact, the ideal sort of man Milner was looking for.

Amery's recommendation was all that Milner needed and he promptly offered Buchan a two-year appointment out on the Cape.

He was to be paid £1,200 per year, a significant sum in those days, although, Buchan was warned, he would have to pay his own fare out to South Africa – a figure in the region of £60.

The whole thing was, Milner declared, something of a gamble but it was an adventure and could be the making of an ambitious young man like himself. Buchan replied to Milner's letter by return, accepting the offer.

Chapter Three

From the Veldt to Border Hunting

When John Buchan arrived in South Africa it was early October 1901 and the Boer War was nearly over. Reconstruction was in the air and Buchan eagerly seized the opportunity to 'do his bit' before everything was tidily packaged up and stored away.

He had formed and retained mixed feelings about the validity of Britain's position during the conflict, commenting that the British Empire might have been in the right – but only just. Now, with hostilities virtually at an end, he was keen to see that everyone, Boers and British alike, were in receipt of the best possible solutions. In his mind no one was to miss out.

Settlers, gold and diamond hunters, industrialists looking for an opportunity to strike it lucky, Buchan found himself mixing with a wide range of men and women. The one thing they all had in common, Buchan included, was a dream of hope and fame. And he quickly became caught up in that powerful vision of a better future for all. However, there were clear problems.

He took one look at the concentration camps that had been established by Lord Kitchener, commander of the British armies during the war, and by other major military figures to hold Boer prisoners and the families of men who had joined the Boer commandoes and was horrified. Like General Kitchener, he never for one moment doubted the effectiveness of the concentration camps but deplored the conditions in which the inmates were forced to live.

He had good reason to be. Men, women and children were starving to death in these disease-ridden establishments, a death rate of 350 per thousand being the overall rate of fatalities. Outbreaks of crippling diseases like scarlet fever and measles ran rampant and nobody seemed to be doing anything to prevent them.

Lord Milner soon turned over responsibility for these camps to Buchan. The young, idealistic Scot could not stomach what he had seen and immediately began to improve sanitation and rations for the prisoners.

Partly as a result of his management – the arrival of doctors and other medical staff from India also helped – by the spring of 1902 the death rate in the camps had fallen to 32 in every thousand. However, the stain of such camps on the British character and on the Imperialist ideal was something that could never be wiped out or eliminated.

Buchan was also responsible for the Transvaal Settlers Ordnances and this involved long rides across the veldt, always with the possibility of encountering elements of De Wet's commandoes, the last throes of Boer resistance. Buchan loved the thrill of danger and the sight and feel of the high veldt.

He particularly enjoyed the high plains and the area to the north of the Drakensberg Mountains, the sweep of the land reminding him of his native hills and valleys in the borders of Scotland. From his earliest encounters with the area, he marked it down as the perfect environment for a future writing project. For the moment, though, he had more than enough to occupy his mind but, incisive as ever, he stored away the images for future use.

Milner had hoped to make the Transvaal and the Orange River State something of a British enclave. It never happened, no more than 12,000 British settlers ever made the territory their homes.[1] It disappointed the young John Buchan but it did not spoil his bubbling enthusiasm for his job.

Buchan was in his element, both when he was out on the veldt and when he was behind his office desk in Johannesburg. He did not like Jo'burg very much, making the sweeping anti-Semitic comment that the city was full of Scots and Jews. It was the first of many anti-Semitic comments that were later to arouse criticism from the reading public.

Johannesburg may not have been to his liking but the work suited him admirably. He was left very much alone, answerable only to Milner. Making decisions and then backing them up with belief and action was ideal for his impetuous soul.

At Oxford, he had looked patronisingly at the college men from the Dominions who, in his opinion, had quickly lost their individuality and drive when faced by the sleepy powers of the university town and life. Out in South Africa, however, he was older, more experienced, and more liable to positive impressions. He soon re-discovered the quality and strength of such men:

> I came in touch with the men of the Dominions – South Africans of the various irregular corps, Canadians, Australians and New Zealanders. Batches of them were seconded to assist me in various jobs, and I had their company in many starlit bivouacs ... I realised that Britain had at least as much to learn from them as they had from Britain.[2]

Milner's young men, whatever their origins, came to be known as *the kindergarten*. It was an accurate enough description, the combination of youth, energy and enthusiasm owned by Buchan and his comrades, men like M R Brand, Basil Blackwood and Hugh Wyndham, being exactly what Milner and the men of power wanted. The friends he made in South Africa would remain friends all his life. More importantly, his experiences would be character-shaping.

It was a robust and exciting period, something which suited Buchan perfectly. He had never been physically strong but out in South Africa, the demands on his energy and bodily strength were exactly what he needed. He had never been fitter, thriving on the work and responsibility.

Buchan met Cecil Rhodes on several occasions. He confessed that he did not like the arch-Imperialist and adventurer very much but could see that he was a 'great man'. Even this opinion Buchan later changed when, with the benefit of emotion recollected in tranquillity, he felt that Rhodes gave off the impression of vast but crippled power. What Rhodes thought of Buchan remains unknown.

Buchan always maintained an admiration for Lord Milner, defending him against criticism and comment for his controversial views and opinions. He never forgot Milner's belief in him, holding it close to his heart for the rest of his days.

***

John Buchan left South Africa in the late summer of 1903, his period of employment with Lord Milner and the government concluded. He had learned and experienced so much, maturing in thought and ideas, but now he had to concentrate on earning his living once more. And that could only be done in England.

What now faced him was a case of going back to the Bar and to the *Spectator* where his old comrade Strachey had guaranteed him an income of £250 a year. It was hardly to be compared with the money he had earned in South Africa but even at this early stage John Buchan knew that his future lay with the written word and it was down to his literary talent if he was going to make a decent living. By the end of 1904, he was writing at least one leader article a week for the paper along with several short notices in each issue.

He was called to the Bar soon after his return from South Africa but found law work uncongenial, mundane and boring after the raw excitement of life in South Africa. As a consequence, apart from a few irregular instances he never really practiced as a lawyer.

At weekends he would head for the country where rock climbing and walking occupied his time. In the evenings, his only real outlet was writing, *The African Colony* – a dramatic and enthralling account of the situation on the Cape – and a long, dull tome on *The Law Relating to the Taxation of Foreign Income* soon appearing under his name.

He was now making important political contacts, regularly 'dining out' with old and new friends and colleagues. Amongst them was R B Haldane, Secretary of State for War, who was then in the process of reorganising the British Army, and the future Field Marshal and commander of the British Expeditionary Force in France, 1914 to 1915, Sir John French.

The most important connection he made, however, was not with politicians and soldiers. It was with Susan Grosvenor, a well-connected and attractive young girl who immediately caught his romantic attention.

Throughout his life, Buchan was conscious of his middle-class background. He was not a snob exactly but he remained very aware, considering the people with whom he mixed, that he was something of an outsider. It is an attitude or emotion that can be seen in virtually all of the leading characters in his novels. Richard Hannay, Edward Leithen, Dickson McCunn, even the nobleman Sandy Arbuthnot are men quite different from the rest of society. They stand alone and apart even when they are, on the surface at least, accepted as good, honest and decent members of their type and class.

Buchan's relationship with Susan Grosvenor went some way to compensating for this feeling of 'difference', although there were many raised eyebrows at the thought of a young girl who was related to several of the great noble families in the land being courted by the son of a mere Free Church Minister from Glasgow.

Buchan proposed to and was accepted by Susan – and her family – in November 1906. If Buchan was well-considered by Susan's family, things were not quite so easy with his own. Mrs Buchan was even more Scottish-centred than her son and was not impressed by an English girl – English of all things – who could barely sew on a button and, more importantly, belonged to another church. Susan was uneasy with Buchan's mother and only what became a life-long friendship with Buchan's sister Anna made the situation bearable for her.

Buchan and Susan were married on 15 July 1907, honeymooning in the Dolomites where he tried to teach her the basics of rock climbing. Susan quickly discovered that she had no head for heights and her education in this particular sport went no further.

On their return, the couple spent some time in Edinburgh. This was not part of the honeymoon, it was business. Buchan's old Oxford friend Tommy Nelson had recently taken over the running of the family publishing business and had asked him to become the firm's literary advisor. The brief Edinburgh sojourn was a case of getting to know the intricacies of the firm's organisation.

Buchan attacked his new job with typical vigour and energy. He launched the firm's Sixpenny Classics Series and the Nelson Sevenpenny Library which saw copyright novels reprinted and republished under the Nelson banner. He was also soon editing *The Scottish Review*, a weekly paper that Nelson's were publishing:

> (This) he soon transformed from a rather parochial affair, much taken up with church matters, into a sort of Scottish *Spectator*.[3]

Buchan worked out of the firm's London offices and took great delight in bringing many of the classics of the past to the notice of the modern reading public. He was particularly pleased to include Erskine Childers' *Riddle of the Sands* in his list, calling it the best story of adventure written in the last hundred years. He was appalled at a suggestion that he should include his own *Sir Quixote of the Moors* in the reprint list, commenting that he had written it at the age of 17 and that it was no more than a piece of juvenilia. He had no wish to see it reprinted – ever!

He was willing, however, to write a new book for Nelson's. This was the work he had been considering and contemplating since his time on the Drakensburg. *Prester John* appeared in 1910 and was the story of Davy Crawford, an idealistic Scottish boy who journeyed to the Transvaal to make his fortune. As might be expected the writing was heavily influenced by Buchan's own time in South Africa with superb descriptions of the veldt and the distant mountains.

Buchan had always been an Imperialist, believing in the benign control and advice of the British Empire, and *Prester John* remains full of racial stereotypes and male chauvinism which fitted easily with those views. In the battle between civilisation and savagery which the book purports to show, the civilisation always comes from the white perspective, the savagery from the native Africans.

All of his life John Buchan retained those Imperialist views, taking particular interest in the Dominions such as South Africa and Canada. It was inevitable that the quirks of Empire, from its in-built racism to the paternalistic concept of 'fatherly' control by Britain, would surface in his writings.

If the topes of racism never quite left him, Buchan's new book was also chock full of adventure and was particularly successful with its depiction of chases and manhunts with which the writer later became synonymous. Buchan regarded *Prester John* as a book for boys but, despite its supposed narrow target audience, it was hugely successful with all elements of society.

He went on to produce two more books for Nelson that year, a life of Walter Raleigh and a biography of one of his childhood heroes, the Marquis of Montrose. He and Susan made their home in Portland Place – a location later made famous as the London dwelling place of one Richard Hannay at the start of *The Thirty-Nine Steps* – but spent most of their weekends at country houses where shooting and dinner parties were the standard order of the day.

In the spring of 1910, despite the heavy calls of book production – not to mention his own writing – the young couple travelled to Constantinople on the Orient Express. Buchan enjoyed rummaging through the bazaars of the city and meeting some of the 'Young Turks' who were in the process of changing Turkish society. It was information and atmosphere that were duly stored away, ready to reappear in what was to be probably his greatest book *Greenmantle*.

Buchan collected more background facts and atmosphere when he and Susan joined Gerard Craig-Sellar, one of his friends from South Africa, for a cruise on his yacht. The trip took them around the Aegean:

> In particular, the sight of a shuttered house in a walled garden by the landing stage of one of the Petali islands, which became the germ of *The Dancing Floor*.[4]

Over the next few years, Buchan and Susan travelled widely. Their destinations included Norway, Bavaria, Germany and France. However, Scotland remained important, both as a holiday destination and as a place of employment when, in 1911, he was elected to Parliament as a Unionist member for Peeblesshire and Selkirk. He enjoyed his time working in the constituency, walking in the hills and talking with the country folk that he met.

In 1912 there was a double tragedy for the family when John Buchan the elder died, worn out by his work in the Gorbals. He was followed to the grave by his son Willie who was struck down with a mysterious sickness whilst on leave from his work and home in India. Helen Buchan, previously the rock in the family, had a nervous collapse but managed to pull through, even though she became a near-invalid for the rest of her life.

All of this took a great toll on John Buchan, first noticed when he began to be troubled by terrible pains in the stomach. He was not one to worry unduly about his health, although he had never been really well since his accident as a child. He tried to ignore the pains but was eventually forced to seek medical advice.

Initially, the trouble was regarded simply as severe indigestion but this diagnosis was soon changed to duodenal ulcers. It was an illness that was to plague him for the rest of his life but even this was to provide Buchan with material for his fiction.

Showing that there was nothing that could not be taken and used by gifted writers, Buchan put his duodenal ulcer to good use. One of his most endearing characters, the American journalist and spy-handler Blenkiron, is suffering from the complaint in *Greenmantle* although he receives a 'miracle cure' in time for his re-appearance in *Mr Standfast*. For Buchan, unfortunately, there was no cure; it was something he simply had to endure.

***

The outbreak of war in August 1914 saw John Buchan seemingly at the pinnacle of his career as a successful politician, as an influential publisher and as a well-regarded writer. He had produced novels, poetry, history and biography at a regular, even surprising, rate but he had not really caught the public eye in the way that his contemporaries, writers like H G Wells and Hilaire Belloc, had managed to do. That was about to change.

The marriage of John and Susan Buchan had been and continued to be a successful one. They were eventually to have four children – Alice, John, William and Alastair, the last two being born during the later war years.

In the summer of 1914 their eldest child, Alice, became ill with mastoid. Sea air was recommended and Susan took Alice, along with John, then their only other child, to Broadstairs for a few weeks' recuperation. They stayed in a house which had an expansive garden and a steep row of steps leading down the cliff face to the beach – as aficionados of *The Thirty-Nine Steps* will know, that sounds more than a little familiar.

Buchan remained in London for a few days but, feeling unwell himself, soon joined his family by the sea. His ulcer had flared up again and bed rest was recommended – a treatment with which Buchan complied. He might be 'resting' in bed but nothing could stop his agile mind running riot as he lay there, bored and restless, gazing at the ceiling. Despite his lethargy and enforced idleness, ideas for two distinctly separate pieces of work came to him.

First was to be a history of the war which, in August 1914, had just begun. It would be published, initially, in fortnightly parts but as the war in its many theatres dragged on this was soon changed to monthly editions. The original idea was to commission Buchan's old friend Hilaire Belloc to write each issue. As it happened Belloc was not available for the job but the idea was a good one, eagerly accepted by Nelson's, and so Buchan was left with no option but to write it himself.

Due to his connections and abilities as a journalist, he was well-placed to gather and analyse all of the facts needed to produce a contemporary account of the war. This was later developed further by the roles he played out during the war years, firstly as a correspondent and then as a government official with his 'fingers in many pies'.

By the end of October 1914, the first part, over 20,000 words of it, had been completed and was sitting safely in the hands of his publisher. It was a massive workload, producing that number of words every month, but it was something that never changed and Buchan was eventually rewarded by seeing all of the constituent parts produced in book form.

The other idea was an altogether more significant enterprise, something that would alter not only his own life but also the habits and tastes of the whole British reading public. It was Buchan's first spy novel, *The Thirty-Nine Steps*.

Previously he had paid scant attention to the spy genre, flitting around the edges of the business in *Prester John* and making the odd comment or two about the origins of spies in *The Power House*, his 1913 serial for *Blackwood's Magazine*. Now, however, he attacked the subject full on.

John Buchan's own words are the best possible way to introduce this revolutionary new book. It comes in the way of a Dedication to his friend and partner in business Tommy Nelson, more of a prelude than a simple dedication. It has continued to be included and precede the text in every single edition of *The Thirty-Nine Steps* that has since been published:

> My Dear Tommy, You and I have long cherished an affection for that elementary type of tale which Americans call "the dime novel," and which we know as the "shocker" – the romance where the incidents defy the probabilities, and march just inside the borders of the possible. During an illness last winter, I exhausted my store of those aids to cheerfulness, and was driven to write one for myself. This little volume is the result, and I should like to put your name on it, in memory of our long friendship, in these days when the wildest fictions are so much less improbable than the facts.[5]

Despite Buchan's self-deprecating and disparaging words, the book was an immediate success. It came out in 1915, published by Blackwood and Sons, a departure from Buchan's normal publishers Nelson who had 'drawn in' their horns on account of the way that the war had virtually wiped out their continental business.

The story, set in the days leading up to the outbreak of war, was exactly what the public wanted, being popular in the home market and with troops in the trenches of Flanders and Picardy. It was Buchan's biggest success so far and has remained the one book of his that everyone knows about and can name.

After a rather convoluted and uneven first chapter, similar in many respects to the first encounter of Sir Edward Leithen and Andrew Lumley in *The Power House*, Buchan found his footing when he sent Hannay off into the hills of Scotland to be pursued by the agents of The Black Stone. The hills and valleys of Lowland Scotland were territory that the writer knew so well and, consequently, the reader was rewarded by the most thrilling piece of spy fiction yet produced:

> It had all the ingredients of the successful spy story – topicality in the midst of war, an exciting chase in which the spy-catcher is pursued by the spy's agents, and a series of cinematic situations amidst splendid background scenery of moor and mountain which made the book a natural for one of Hitchcock's best films of the Thirties.[6]

The Thirty-Nine Steps was a relatively short book, probably one of the reasons for its success with the soldiers in France, men who had little time or inclination to read long and deep. It is notable for a total absence of female characters – another reason, perhaps, for its popularity with the soldiery? – thus making it a man's book written by a man and intended essentially for male consumption.

Alfred Hitchcock and the three other film directors who later came to make movies of the book had to change this aspect of the story in order to make it fit the classic 'thriller bill' but the changes, when they came, did not worry Buchan unduly. He often said that Hitchcock's film and the changes he made to the plot-line and characters simply improved the story.

Subsequent film directors continued to use Hitchcock's alterations to the original text as well as making a few more changes or additions of their own – Hannay hanging beneath the Forth Bridge or swinging off the clock hands of Big Ben; a climax which involves a shooting in a London music hall and so on. The one thing that remained the same in every filmed version of the story – four in number at the time of writing – was the inclusion of a strong female character.

Richard Hannay, at this stage of his fictional existence a spy-hunter rather than a spy, has gone on to become an icon in the world of spy fiction. He was the perfect hero for the time, a man of personal courage and clear moral standards, albeit with the Union

Jack metaphorically stamped across his forehead. Buchan went on to write better books but none of them has ever quite grabbed the public imagination so clearly and so succinctly as *The Thirty-Nine Steps*. The book has never gone out of print and with Buchan now out of copyright that is hardly likely to change.

Buchan's best-seller was not without its faults. The explanatory opening chapter where Scudder spins Hannay a web of lies and half-truths in order to gain his attention and his help, is convoluted and contrived. Face-to-face conversation might be one thing – and was undoubtedly something at which the erudite Buchan excelled – but, on the printed page, debating policy and abstract concepts like nihilism and anarchy were simply not his strength.

In his writing, as in his life, John Buchan was always better when describing action scenes. The opening chapter of *The Thirty-Nine Steps* is obviously necessary. Without it, the whole plot line would have imploded but once Hannay takes the train north the book really comes into its own. The scenes where the hunted and haunted hero is fleeing through the heather with the police and the villains of the piece on his heels have rarely been done better.

However, there are other faults, particularly in the opening scenes. Once again there are clear racist undertones in the book, particularly a strong strain of anti-Semitism. It cannot be ignored or excused but such attitudes were typical of the time when he was writing, so perhaps he may be allowed a degree of latitude in these views?

It is interesting to note that despite the anti-Semitic nature of some of Buchan's writing he was a confirmed supporter of Zionism and later publicly denounced Hitler's anti-Semitic policies in Germany. None of that can ever excuse some of the quite rabid comments he made in books like *The Thirty-Nine Steps* but neither should it be allowed to detract from the excitement and the energy of the writing.

Whatever its faults, in the years after 1915 the book became a trendsetter and many writers have since gone on record regarding the debt they owe to John Buchan. *The Thirty-Nine Steps* changed the world of spy fiction, taking the product of William Le Queux and other early exponents of the art and turning it on its head, making nearly all previous attempts at establishing a genre utterly redundant and out of date.

Buchan's book has become almost a manual or a template for how to write spy stories. There have since been dozens of books where the hero uncovers a plot and then becomes a hunted man – or woman – as the enemy agents try to track him down and kill him. It is a simple enough format but there is no denying the fact that it works exceedingly well.

***

John Buchan's poor health meant that he had little hope of seeing any active service during the war years. His age was also against him. Buchan was not best pleased but accepted his confinement with a degree of resignation.

Arguably he performed his best service for his country by writing *Nelson's History of the War*, an enterprise that occupied him from 1914 until the war's end in 1918. However, Buchan being Buchan, he had other ideas of how he might help his country.

When he was approached by *The Times* and asked to visit the trenches as their Special Correspondent, he leapt at the chance. He had never lost that love of adventure which had taken him to South Africa and which then surfaced in the pages of *The Thirty-Nine Steps*. So, to be in France where the youth of the country were fighting for their lives and for the Empire was the fulfilment of his every wish.

By May 1915 he was in Flanders and had soon written half a dozen articles for the paper. He pulled no punches, stressing the German superiority in armaments and weapons and noting, in particular, the British shortage of artillery shells. This was a problem that did not go away, despite Buchan's observations. It certainly hindered the British assault on the Somme in 1916 and was not solved until David Lloyd

George took charge of munitions and the provision of decent artillery shells.

Buchan was back in France in the autumn of 1915, reporting on the Battle of Loos. He was now the recipient of a Field Commission, holding the rank of Lieutenant in the Army Intelligence Corps. It was not long before he was promoted to Major and then Lieutenant Colonel.

He was attached to the staff of Field Marshal Haig, the new commander of the BEF, until the succession of Lloyd George to the position of Prime Minister in December 1916 gave him greater opportunities to use his talents. Buchan had clashed with the fiery little Welshman several times, notably across the floor of the Commons, but he never doubted Lloyd George's ability to bring the war to a successful conclusion.

At the urging of Lloyd George and Lord Alfred Milner – who was now in the new PM's War Cabinet – Buchan took up a position in the recently reformed Department of Information, literally Britain's first Propaganda Bureau. For a man of Buchan's intellect and background, it was a perfect way to 'do his bit' for the war effort and to help with the defeat of Kaiser Wilhelm.

In the new Department of Information, Buchan worked closely with Charles Masterman, a fellow MP and the original founder of Britain's Propaganda Bureau. Buchan considered him one of the most able but, at the same time, one of the most misunderstood civil servants of the war. When Masterman was later side-lined in favour of men like Lord Northcliffe and Lord Beaverbrook, Buchan continued to work in the propaganda field but considered his years 'post-Masterman' as some of the hardest times of his life!

While Buchan could not physically fight the German war machine, he was appalled at the toll the war took on his friends. His Oxford compatriot Raymond Asquith, son of the Prime Minister, had fallen on the Somme in 1916 and then at the Battle of Arras the following year his great friend and business partner Tommy Nelson, the dedicatee of

The Thirty-Nine Steps, was also killed. The same battle saw the death of Buchan's brother Alastair.

All around him, it seemed, friends and family were being cut down, killed or wounded. Buchan, sensitive and caring, could do nothing to help the grieving families but he took the stresses and strains on himself. Inevitably, the pressures affected his physical health and right through the war years, he suffered terribly from his duodenal ulcer.

Buchan continued to work for the Propaganda Bureau and, as the war went on, spent more and more time embroiled with the organisers of Britain's secret policies:

> I rubbed shoulders with a great variety of human beings. I added to my already extensive military acquaintance, and in London I had to concern myself with every variety of social and political groups, while one side of my duties brought me into touch with the queer subterranean world of the Secret Service ... I met every foreigner of importance who came to London. I saw something of the veiled prophets who are behind the scenes in a crisis.[7]

How directly involved he was in the business of spying remains unclear. He was never a spy himself but he certainly had his fingers on the pulse of the secret world. The extent of this remains unknown. It was not something that he spoke readily about.

His work for the propaganda arm of the British government brought him close to all sorts of hidden operations and mysterious but fascinating individuals. These ranged from little-known figures like spies and agents to government officials and high-ranking Allied officers.

As far as Buchan was concerned, his career in the Ministry of Information became important work, essential in the winning of the war. However, more significantly for his career as a writer, it gave him valuable experiences in and around the clandestine world of espionage, experiences that he could and would tap on when needed.

For all of his life, John Buchan retained the remarkable ability to store away his experiences, in war-time and when the world was at peace, and use them in his future spy novels. The value and art of propaganda, for example, was one of the central themes of his post-war Hannay adventure *The Three Hostages*.

If there is one downside to his involvement with the government at this time it was simply that he could not be as critical of the leadership – both in his novels and in his *History of the War* – as he would have liked to be. The quality of the writing more than makes up for this deficit.

Chapter Four

A World of Spies

Throughout the war John Buchan continued to write fiction, the spy genre becoming ever more interesting for him. Considering his other duties for the war effort it is amazing to think that as well as his Richard Hannay stories, he continued to produce 20,000 words every month on the history and course of the war. It was pressure and strain that would have killed lesser men.

His greatest book and perhaps his ultimate contribution to the genre of spy writing came in the immediate sequel to *The Thirty-Nine Steps*. This was the dramatic thriller *Greenmantle* which appeared first in serial form in 1916 and was set in various parts of war-torn Europe and the Middle East. Not as well-known as the earlier thriller, *Greenmantle* was an immediate best-seller, gaining and retaining immense popularity.

It was the sections of the book set in Constantinople and the surrounding country that appealed to the reading public but Hannay's adventures in the Bavarian forests and on the barges of the Danube are also riveting in their accuracy and excitement. The appeal of the book was so great that it remains the only one of Buchan's books to have outsold *The Thirty-Nine Steps*.

Hannay becomes a spy in *Greenmantle* – rather than the spy-catcher of the earlier book – tracking down the source of a German plot to foment revolution in the Middle East.

He has only a three-word clue – 'Kasredin, cancer and v.I' – the cryptic message having been scrawled on a piece of paper by the dying son of Sir Walter Bullivant. He also has the chilling warning that trouble is brewing in the East. Bullivant offers Hannay the choice, take the task or return to his Regiment with promotion to the rank of Brigadier. For Hannay, of course, there is no real choice.

From this unpromising start where he has no real idea of where to go or what to do, Hannay begins to pick up the traces and begins his adventure. He is aided by the American John Scantlebury Blenkiron, by his aristocratic outsider friend Sandy Arbuthnot and by Boer adventurer Peter Pienaar. They disperse to go their separate ways and uncover what they can before meeting again in Constantinople a month later.

Ever conscious of the real war which was still raging as he wrote, Buchan plotted his book to culminate with the recent Russian victory over Turkish forces at Erzurum in Anatolia. He was immediately faced with a problem of logistics. He had never been further east than Constantinople and so he cleverly relied on the elements, principally snow and fog, to disguise what were really the Scottish hills and the veldt of South Africa – both of which he knew exceedingly well – and which provide the sense of place which makes the final section of the book so memorable.

Greenmantle remains an unusual spy novel, unusual at least for John Buchan. There are chases and gun fights in plenty but it is in the characters of the two chief villains and in a series of brief but intense character sketches that Buchan scores heavily:

> In the person of Hilda von Einem there is rather more sex than is usual in a Buchan thriller. There are hints of deviancy in von Stumm. The character sketches of the Kaiser, Enver Pasha and Grand Duke Nicholas are quick, sharp and humane.[1]

Hilda von Einem is the first really effective female character in any Buchan book. She is mysterious, dangerous and uses her sexual power to draw Sandy into her web. Von Stumm has clear homosexual tendencies which Buchan only hints at – and therefore makes all the more effective – in his creation of the otherwise gross personality of the German agent. Whereas Hilda von Einem is a whisp of a figure, her translucence serving to build and aid her sexual appeal, von Stumm is a particularly menacing figure for Hannay to confront and finally defeat.

The short character sketches of the Kaiser and other real-life individuals are surprisingly humane, considering that many of them were, at that time, enemies of Britain and her allies. Buchan in the guise of Richard Hannay is moved to comment feelingly of the Kaiser that he would not have been 'in his shoes for the throne of the Universe.'

Needless to say, Hannay decodes the mysterious message and eventually defeats the machinations of Hilda von Einem and Colonel von Stumm. It is a masterful book, full of twists and turns that make the reader feel at one with the British espionage agents.

The exotic locations for the book are brilliantly drawn, reminiscent in some respects of the earlier work of Le Queux and others who set their novels on the North-West Frontier and in other entrancing places. In reality, however, Buchan's writing is far, far superior. Buchan's quality and command of the English language shines through in what has remained his most effective and most powerful piece of writing.

John Buchan's third spy novel of the Great War is *Mr Standfast*. It was written in 1917-18 but not published until 1919, a year after the war had ended. It is the darkest of his Hannay books, several of the leading characters being killed off at the end – in keeping with the recurring theme and links to Bunyan's *Pilgrim's Progress*. Hannay's companions Peter Pienaar and Launcelot Wake are doomed to die but theirs is a valiant sacrifice, a sacrifice which will ensure their eventual ennoblement in the Puritan preacher Bunyan's vision of Paradise.

Mr Standfast is really a book of two halves. Hannay is once more pulled back from his battalion and despatched on a secret mission tracking down a German spy ring. His travels take him into familiar territory, notably a trek across the Isle of Skye, and send him fleeing for his life across the Scottish hills ahead of the pursuing German agents. A chance encounter with the chief German spy, variously called Moxon Ivery, Clarence Donne and Graf Otto von Schwabing, during a London air raid reveals him to be Hannay's old foe, the leader of the Black Stone who escaped capture at the end of *The Thirty-Nine Steps*.

The second part of the book sees Hannay back at the Front. There, with the aid of Mary Lamington and John Blenkiron, he thwarts the German plot but only after breakneck car races and an almost impossible traverse of the Swiss Mountains. Mary is Hannay's love interest but she is also the object of desire by the German agent and, equally as hopelessly, of conscientious objector Launcelot Wake.

Mr Standfast takes several of the themes touched on in *Greenmantle* and further develops them – notably the strong female character of Mary. She has many of the traits of Hilda von Einem about her but, unlike the villain of *Greenmantle,* Mary is clear about her beliefs and her support of what she (and Hannay) perceives as right. She is beautiful but also strong-willed, the perfect life companion for Hannay. Even so, she still needs his strong arm in order to survive the machinations of Moxon Ivery/von Schwabing.

The character of Peter Pienaar – the Mr Standfast of the title – is well drawn, in contrast to his appearance in *Greenmantle* where he is little more than an extra with little to contribute to the plot line or the unravelling of the secret. His heroic death, crashing his aeroplane into the German fighter ace Lensch, thereby killing them both, provides a momentous ending to the book.

Similarly, Blenkiron is a considerably more substantial figure in *Mr Standfast* than he was in the earlier book. He appears here, his duodenal ulcer cured, as the spymaster who directs Hannay's efforts and plots von Schwabing's downfall, using Hannay's raw courage and defiance to power the Allies through to a successful climax.

***

After the war, Buchan and his family moved to Elsfield Manor in the Cotswolds. The similarity of Elsfield to Fosse Manor, the house where Mary gives Hannay his first instructions in *Mr Standfast*, is remarkable, almost as if Buchan was attempting to create a real-life version of his fiction. For once it is not a case of Buchan drawing on his memories and past experiences; here, for the first time, he takes a fictional location from one of his spy stories and makes it reality.

Buchan continued to write his spy novels, notably *Huntingtower* where his new creation of Dickson McCunn, a retired Glasgow grocer, takes on and defeats the agents of communist Russia – all to help a damsel in distress who is literally locked up in a tower on the Scottish coast.

The book is notable for several reasons. Firstly, it is a far more romantic version of the spy story than any of the Hannay tales, in keeping with the post-war feelings and emotions of the nation. A little light romance, combined with exciting spy material was exactly what the people of Britain wanted. It was, you might say, a forerunner, albeit a less-explicit one, of Ian Fleming's James Bond books of the 1950s and 1960s.

Then there was the invention of the Gorbals Die-Hards, a group of ruffians from the Gorbals area in Glasgow. This was a creation of pure genius, the platoon of Glasgow children being yet another example of 'outsiders' who turn out to be a necessary element in the successful outcome of the story. Important or central to the plot they might be but, at the same time, they manage to happily continue with their position on the fringes of society.

The Die-Hards are a poverty-stricken group of boys who form themselves into a Scout Troop, Buchan clearly drawing on his experiences in the Gorbals as a teenager. The Die-Hards are aided in their attempts to better themselves by the philanthropic Dickson McCunn who funds them in their enterprise. The Gorbals Die-Hards, in turn, help him to defend the heroine in Huntingtower House. They suffer badly at the hands of the Russian agents but stick with their task to the end – in the best traditions of the Boy Scouts.

In the characters of Dougal, the Die-Hards leader and a boy with a brain two or three times more effective than might be expected, and of Wee Jaikie, the smallest member of the group who always cries before he actually hits anyone, Buchan managed to draw stunning portraits of bravery supplanting breeding. Interestingly, Buchan himself was always interested in scouting and later in his career as a Diplomat became Chief Scout for Canada.

The book was immensely popular with the reading public and, consequently, Mr McCunn appeared in two more Buchan stories along with several of the Gorbals Die-Hards. The books were well-received – particularly *Castle Gay* which opens with a riveting description of an international rugby match – but neither of them had quite the romantic spy novel feel of Huntingtower.

Popular demand forced Buchan to bring Hannay out of retirement in *The Three Hostages* and *The Island of Sheep* but these were both pure thrillers rather than spy stories. As ever, Buchan relied heavily on his own life experiences to provide the background for these books:

> There was a new one (new book) every year from 1922 to 1936; many of them, from *The Three Hostages* to *The Island of Sheep*, reflected the pleasures and activities of the Buchans' holidays during these years; climbing and stalking and fishing in Mull and Morvern and Wester Ross; fishing and bird watching (with Johnnie outstripping his father as an ornithologist) in the Shetlands and Faeroes.[2]

As ever, in these post-war years Buchan's activities outside writing were keeping him well occupied. In a by-election in 1927 he became the Unionist Party MP for the Scottish Universities but also found time to take up other duties such as President of the Exploration Club and Treasurer of the Conservative Association. He made new friends, notably T E Lawrence and Robert Graves.

For many years people believed that the character of Richard Hannay had been based on T E Lawrence, Lawrence of Arabia as he was universally known. Reputation, yes, character, no. Lawrence's exploits did not become familiar to the public until after the first two Hannay books had been published. In truth, Hannay was an amalgam of several characters, perhaps most significantly General Edmund Ironside who Buchan had met in South Africa when the General was operating as a spy during the Boer War.

In 1933 Buchan became High Commissioner to the General Assembly of the Church of Scotland. It was a largely honorific position; the work, such as it was, being confined to just two weeks of the year when Buchan lived at Holyrood Palace and spent his time opening fetes and making speeches. It was, however, a hint at what was soon to come.

In 1935 he was invited to take up the post of High Commissioner for Canada. The invitation came directly from the Canadian Prime Minister, W L Mackenzie King, a procedure that had been established in 1910, long before the war. However, Buchan was a commoner and King George V was nothing if not a traditionalist. If Buchan was to take the Office, he would have to be ennobled.

On 1 June 1934, he was elevated to the peerage as Baron Tweedsmuir of Elsfield. He may have been happy about his peerage but Buchan was not sure about the Canadian post, feeling that it would intrude on his other interests. And yet he believed implicitly in the concept of Empire and Dominions. He was torn and undecided but Susan Buchan went one step further; she hated the whole idea of living a life in the public eye. The only member of the family who was happy was Buchan's mother. 'The King is fortunate to get you,' she declared.

In the end, duty overcame reservations. Regardless of his concerns, John Buchan, newly created Baron Tweedsmuir, sailed for Canada, duly arriving on 2 November 1935.

From the beginning of his time in office, he was a much-loved High Commissioner, forming a lasting relationship with the Canadian people and with Prime Minister Mackenzie King. He toured widely, traversing the country several times, and seeming, to the Canadian people, to have the common touch that was so crucial for the position. And despite their concerns, both Buchan and his wife thoroughly enjoyed the job.

The Canadian outback had great appeal to him, reminding him of South Africa and the Scottish hills and mountains. The official residence of the High Commissioner was in Ottawa but he was often to be found in the outback, fishing or hunting. The most taxing of his duties was the visit of the King and his family in 1939, although official policy dictated that he remained very much 'in the background' during the visit.

He continued to write, being heavily influenced by the warmth and sincerity of the Canadian people and the vastness of the country. The whole Canadian experience was similar in many respects to his earlier time in South Africa and Buchan saw it as a country where youth and vitality shone.

He did not have premonitions of death, at least not explicitly or exactly, seeing himself as being still a young man. However, he did approach the theme of dying in his last completed novel:

> If Buchan had a setting (the North) and his theme (dying), he needed a character. Of the personnel of his thrillers Richard Hannay was too hale, Archie Roylance too boisterous, Lord Lamancha too shadowy, Dickson McCunn too commercial, Sandy Clanroyden too heroic. That left the lawyer, Sir Edward Leithen, devised thirty years ago – for the short story "Space" (1912) – when Buchan himself was trying to make his way at the London Bar.[3]

Sick Heart River did duly record the death of Edward Leithen, out of all of his many creations the character most like Buchan himself.

With a confirmed diagnosis of impending death, Leithen seeks solace and acceptance in the wild northern wilderness of Canada. His decline and the inevitability of his fate are probably amongst the most powerful pieces of writing Buchan ever produced:

> He was moved to a strange exaltation. Behind his new access of strength, he felt the brittleness of his body. His stock of vigour was slender indeed but he could spend it bravely in making his soul. Most men had their lives taken from them. It was his privilege to give his, to offer it freely and joyfully in one last effort of manhood.[4]

That was probably the best epitaph John Buchan could ever have written for himself. It was almost over. All that was left was his memoir and autobiography *Memory Hold the Door* which duly appeared the year before his death.

There was little introspection in *Memory Hold the Door* which is a glorious recall of incidents and people. Indeed, there is far more analysis of his life and various careers in *Sick Heart River* than there ever is in his autobiography.

On Tuesday 6 November 1940 John Buchan suffered a slight stroke whilst shaving. He fell backwards onto the bathroom floor, hitting his head. Unconscious and bleeding, he was not found for an hour. He was rushed to hospital where he recovered consciousness and seemed to be improving. It was a false dawn as pressure on the brain began to increase. He lapsed again into unconsciousness and despite two subtemporal operations, he died on the evening of Sunday 11 November 1940.

***

So, where does that leave John Buchan in the pantheon of espionage writers? He had no false modesty and regarded his biographies and histories as more significant pieces of work than any of his spy fiction. A writer is rarely the best judge of his own work, however, and Buchan undoubtedly under-valued his fictional output.

In his five strongest novels – *Greenmantle, Mr Standfast, The Thirty-Nine Steps, Huntingtower* and *Sick Heart River*, books which I rank in that order – he created fictional worlds that brought his readers up short and which continue to weave a web of delight for anyone who reads them today. They are, perhaps, of their time but even now they still hold a message for the readers – courage and strength of purpose are the most important elements in the characters of men and women.

Let me be personal for a moment – after all, this is a very personal choice of greatness! A little while ago I led a creative writing workshop for young people, all of them under the age of eighteen. We were looking at the process of writing reviews and, as part of the course, watched the Alfred Hitchcock film version of *The Thirty-Nine Steps*. The youngsters then went off to read the book before coming back with their completed reviews of book and film. Every single one of them was clear – the book was 100% better than the film. Buchan's words, it seemed, had held their power.

There is really no comparison between Buchan and the spy novelists who preceded him – with the one exception of Erskine Childers and he wrote only one book of real note. John Buchan did it time after time, rarely producing anything that was not of exceptional quality.

What he also did was to create a whole new style of spy fiction where the main and minor characters, all of the significant players in each book, are as important as the plot. So, too, is the location, the setting of the story.

You cannot say or even think of *Greenmantle* or *The Thirty-Nine Steps* without the character of Richard Hannay immediately coming to mind. And it's the same with *Huntingtower* where Dickson McCunn is the main and most memorable figure. Say *Mr Standfast* and what quickly surfaces are the wild mountains of Skye and the trenches on the Western Front where Hannay and his Battalion make their last stand. *Sick Heart River* stands and falls on its depiction of the northern territories of Canada. I could go on.

Suffice to say that what John Buchan understood, far better than almost any of the spy writers who went before him, was that the three p's were – and remain – crucially important in the creation of popular fiction.

The three p's? Place, people and problem. The third p – problem – is vital with spy stories but to give it too much emphasis is to create a bland and unfulfilling piece of fiction. Out of good characters and a good sense of place will come sense of purpose or problem – in other words, plot! And that was something which John Buchan understood only too well.

Beginning with *The Thirty-Nine Steps* Buchan created a series of books filled with small cameos, brief encounters between his hero Richard Hannay and people who help or hinder him in his mission. So, in *The Thirty-Nine Steps*, we have a whole brigade of them – the Literary Innkeeper, the Radical Candidate, the Spectacled Roadman, the Bald Archaeologist and the Dry Fly Fisherman, all of which lead us inevitably to the Coming of the Black Stone.

Some of the encounters – the Literary Innkeeper and so on – are self-contained and once over are consigned to memory. Others like the Bald Archaeologist and the Dry Fly Fisherman are central to the continuation and final working out of the story. They are all, however, perfect little interactions which create reader interest through the characters and the places they inhabit.

It was a technique that Buchan continued to use in all his spy novels, notably *Greenmantle* where Hannay, fever-ridden and almost at his wit's end, is fleeing for his life through the Bavarian forests. Deep in the frozen wastes of the woods, he stumbles upon a remote cottage where the woman of the house, her husband a German soldier away at the war, gives him shelter and succour. In return, he befriends her and her children, all thoughts of helping the enemy and the fraternisation which is taking place are ignored – by both sides.

Hannay goes on to make a similar encounter with the skipper of a barge fleet on the Danube and, in a curious twist of fate, helps carry the ammunition that will soon be used against his colleagues and fellow soldiers at Gallipoli and Kut.

In delivering the shells to the German gunners Hannay runs up against the villainous Rasta the Turk before, in the back streets of Constantinople, meeting with the Companions of the Rosy Hours. Once again, these are all perfect sketches where the individual players remain in your memory long after the book has been laid aside. That applies whether, like the German wife in the forest they never appear again or, as with Rasta, they return to haunt Hannay and his friends several times.

One lesson that Buchan, possibly, learned from Erskine Childers was the need to include detail in his stories. Not just detail but masses and masses of it.

All of his spy novels are not only packed with information about codes, military tactics and world affairs, they are also full of what, at first glance, might seem superfluous information but which, on second or third look, give the writing that extra sense of class which other novelists of Buchan's type seem to lack. And yet it does not detract from the adventure or the pace of the book.

Some of it is not really noticeable unless you start out to look for it. For example, there really is a house on the cliffs at Broadstairs which has thirty-nine steps leading down to the sea! The hidden cove on the Isle of Skye where Hannay bathes in *Mr Standfast* does actually exist. And so on. The reader does not need to know any of this but real places, real locations that Buchan had seen and experienced, give credibility and make the writing doubly impressive.

As for the espionage writers who came after him, John Buchan created a model that they could follow. The key word in that sentence is 'could'.

Sadly, too many chose to concentrate simply on the action found in Hannay's adventures but they did it without having the finer points of his creator's skill. Sapper's *Bulldog Drummond*, apart from the snobbery, racism, violence and sexism displayed in the stories, is probably the classic example of how to get it wrong, how to take Buchan's worst points and totally ignore the good:

> The advent of the First World War whetted the appetite of the reading public for this kind of thing and the spy story became a habit rather than a cult. Some of the stories were competent, one or two like Maugham's *Ashenden* were first class, the vast majority was mediocre and many more appallingly bad, both as credible plots and as examples of the written word.[5]

Somerset Maugham, Graham Greene and Eric Ambler were exceptions to the long list of second-rate spy novelists who followed in Buchan's footsteps. Indeed, in my personal list of preferences all three were in my 'Top Ten' and came close to featuring in the highest echelon.

Maugham, Greene and Ambler were writers who, with their attention to detail and characterisation, succeeded in producing work which almost matched that of John Buchan. Certainly, all three men produced thoughtful but tense thrillers which stand the test of time and scrutiny. The three of them, each in their own way, went on to pave the ground for Fleming and le Carré in the years after the Second World War.

Greene wrote only a handful of spy novels, notably books like *Our Man in Havana* – possibly the best tongue-in-cheek and satirical espionage book ever written – *The Quiet American* and *Ministry of Fear*. His best-known and perhaps most effective thriller, *The Third Man*, is not really a spy story at all but it has strong espionage overtones and in the words of Donald McCormick is set in post-World War Two Vienna, the classic 'spy city'.[6]

Graham Greene openly admitted that the influence of John Buchan was integral to his success. Yet there remains a question mark about his credentials as a spy writer. Is he a writer of spy fiction or a writer who uses the espionage business to carry the story that he really wants to tell? I suspect the latter but the jury remains out.

Eric Ambler only really came to prominence in 1938 with the publication of *Epitaph for a Spy* but he was probably the main participant in the unofficial movement or drive for the removal of Sapper et al from the minds of the reading public. Again, he was a writer whose main concern was not to tell an espionage story but to relay an account of the individual problems facing his 'hero' – which might well involve things like mistaken identity and the fringes of espionage. In almost all of Ambler's books, the art and practice of spying takes second place to his interest in human relationships.

His central characters are not spies but ordinary men and women who, by circumstance or by bad judgement, find themselves caught up in a web of deceit and danger from which they occasionally emerge to encounter spies and spying.

What Ambler does, more than any other writer of his era, is to show that in that world of espionage there is really no such thing as bad or good. In Ambler's various books and stories, there is no right or wrong, just people caught and held – sometimes destroyed – by fate.

Out of these three significant writers the one who comes closest to Buchan, if not in style, then certainly in effect is the one who was closest to him in age and education – William Somerset Maugham.

Maugham's hero Ashenden is not someone like Richard Hannay, a dashing figure complete with stiff upper lip, but an ordinary little man who is plagued by ordinary fears and by ordinary human desires. As such, he has more in common with the George Smiley contingent than he ever does with James Bond, Richard Hannay and other secret agents of his time:

> Ashenden was no brilliant performer of courageous deeds: he worried about missing trains and had an attack of nerves when a fellow agent was about to murder a Greek spy ... The realism of *Ashenden* contrasted markedly with the heroics and melodrama, the high-life of Oppenheim and Le Queux.[7]

He might have been the polar opposite of Sapper, Le Queux and the others but Maugham still took much from the work of his main contemporary and leading exponent of the spy novel, John Buchan. Attention to detail, love of foreign places, tiny cameos that hold the story together and push the plot forward are all as important to Maugham as they are to Buchan.

There is a feeling of reality in his *Ashenden*, the events he describes being similar in many ways to *The Thirty-Nine Steps* or *Greenmantle*, albeit without the heroics. They are, however, equally as compelling and riveting in style. That is what separates him from the mass of poor spy writers who were pursuing and pushing their 'art' in the 1930s.

In his portrayal of the spy Ashenden as a quiet and mild-mannered little man who is intent on doing his duty in as unobtrusive a way as possible, Somerset Maugham was something of a trendsetter himself. He would hardly have recognised the phrase 'trendsetter', his portrayal of the quiet but effective spy being little more than a reproduction of his own personality.

Influenced by Buchan? There is no doubt about that. Yet the real significance of Somerset Maugham as a writer of spy tales was at the other end of the spectrum. It is as an influence on Deighton, Le Carré and many other modern spy novelists that he is best remembered and where he carried out his best, most effective piece of work. He remains a highly significant writer of espionage fiction and holds a position of excellence all on his own.

Chapter Five

Ian Fleming, Bond Alive

In many respects Ian Fleming is the one spy novelist whose name everyone will know and remember but will probably dismiss as being insignificant in terms of literary achievement and standing. If that is so, then the ubiquitous 'everyone' is probably being disingenuous and maybe even a little priggish.

The overnight success of *Casino Royale*, Fleming's first book, selling its way out of print within a month of its appearance, proved that this was no 'one-hit wonder'. This was a writer to note and remember.

Public acclaim and high sales of both hardback and paperback volumes of his work continued for the rest of Ian Fleming's life – and beyond! In addition to the books sold during his working life, two volumes of his Bond stories were published posthumously. So was his children's tale *Chitty-Chitty-Bang-Bang* and a dozen or so Bond-style stories commissioned from other writers by publishers who did not want to lose out in the guaranteed success stakes that any book which bore the Bond tag would offer. These books were written by eminent novelists like Kingsley Amis, John Gardner and Sebastian Faulks.

During the 1950s and '60s Fleming was probably the bestselling author of the age and in 2008 readers of *The Times* newspaper voted him 14th in its list of the greatest British writers since the end of the Second World War. That is no mean accolade.

If, in your opinion, status is achieved by things like public voting, league tables and so on, being ranked as the 14th best writer since 1945 was, and still is, something that has to lodge Fleming fairly high up in the pantheon of successful authors.

If nothing else this notice of appreciation surely places Fleming on a par with John Buchan whose third Richard Hannay novel *Mr Standfast* was, in 2009, voted by the BBC to a high position in the Top 100 most influential novels of the previous century. Such a comparison to Buchan was something which would have undoubtedly pleased Ian Fleming.

Those are interesting rankings but, arguably, such voting and listing are irrelevant. What matters is audience appreciation and, in this Ian Fleming, whose Bond novels have sold over 100 million copies worldwide, surely reigns supreme as a quality literary figure.

During the 1960s everyone in the western world – and behind the Iron Curtain, too – had read at least one Bond book. As far as teenagers like myself were concerned, it would be fair to say that we waited avidly for the next paperback to appear on the shelves of W H Smith or other book sellers. And when, in 1962, the first Bond movie – *Dr No*, not *Casino Royale* which was the first novel – hit the cinema's screens it was a landmark moment in the year.

Fleming apparently had doubts about the potential success of the films; the public did not. Bond, as caught on the cinema screen by Sean Connery, and the early film scripts were, the public felt, a perfect match. Interestingly, when *Dr No* did finally appear Fleming was to change his mind about the films and their potential both as money-making materials and as contributions to the art of cinema. He did not live to see the gimmick-ridden films of Roger Moore and other future Bond's but, given his liking for trick weapons he would probably have approved.

The 1960s was a time of new dawning. Gone were the drab, depressing post-war days when food was short, when luxury goods meant, if you were lucky, an extra blanket for the bed. Prime Minister Harold Macmillan might declare that the British people had never had it so good but it was a statement that nobody under the age of twenty ever really believed. And everyone looked eagerly ahead for the changes that were bound to come. When those changes came, they erupted with sudden vitality which took everyone by surprise.

Clothing designed specifically for teenagers, music from the Beatles and other evolutionary bands, access to foreign travel and exotic locations, even if it was just Marbella or Majorca – it was all suddenly available to a public that was desperate to snap it all up. It was a time to be young and to experience all that was now suddenly on offer.

It was also perhaps inevitable that the reading matter of the age did not just keep up with the changes but actually set the trends. Ian Fleming found a voice with his up-market secret agent and he exploited it beautifully.

***

Ian Lancaster Fleming was born in the Mayfair district of London on 28 May 1908. His family was closely connected to the banking industry, being owners of Robert Fleming and Co., wealthy merchant bankers, and the early years of the boy's life were, one might safely say, enjoyed in what were quite luxurious surroundings.

For a brief period before the First World War, the family lived at Pitt House at Braziers Park in Oxford while Fleming's father, Valentine Fleming, was Member of Parliament for Henley and South Oxfordshire. His mother, Evelyn 'Eve' St Croix Fleming, nee Rose, was a strikingly beautiful woman who won the admiration of almost everyone she met.

Despite their seemingly 'Home Counties' background, the family origins were Scottish, the patriarch Robert having originated from Dundee where he was a self-made man who hauled himself up by his shoe laces! It was a background of which the family remained inordinately proud.

Their Scottish origins were repeatedly drummed into Ian and his elder brother Peter and, latterly, the two youngest Fleming boys

Richard and Michael. 'Never forget – you are not English, you're Scottish,' Eve Fleming used to say. It was a message that Ian chose to ignore, at least until much later in his life.

His mother's presence and latent – sometimes actual – power were significant. She was widowed in 1917 when her husband, then a Major commanding a unit of the Queen's Own Oxfordshire Hussars, was killed by German artillery shelling. She was left financially well provided for but with the responsibility of raising four young children while still a young woman herself.

By the terms of Valentine Fleming's will his widow was, perhaps for the first time in her life, made independent and wealthy. Whether or not Valentine deliberately chose to clamp her into a metaphorical straight jacket is not clear but Eve Fleming would have been guilty of financial suicide if she had ever re-married. She would have lost her capital along with her income and the substantial property portfolio which Valentine had bequeathed her.

Eve Fleming was nothing if not a pragmatist. The terms and conditions of her husband's will did not stop her from engaging in a long-term relationship with the bohemian artist Augustus John, with whom she had an illegitimate daughter named Amaryllis. It was probably pure coincidence but both Ian Fleming and Augustus John were also to have children named Caspar!

Under Eve Fleming's strict control, it was a very 'Victorian' upbringing for Ian and his brothers but, almost from the beginning, his mother discovered that there was a rebellious streak in her second son. If he saw authority or control, he would challenge it at every opportunity. School, Mrs Fleming believed, would change him. She was wrong.

Durnford Preparatory School on the Isle of Purbeck in Dorset was a typical pre-public school establishment where young boys were prepared for life in private education. It was a world of privilege and plenty, even if it was rigid in its approach to headstrong and self-willed youths. It was Ian Fleming's first taste of formal education and he hated it from the start. He was seven years old when he arrived at the school and with his dislike of authority and all its representatives, it was inevitable that he would come up, nose to nose, with people and regimes that would challenge his view on life.

Strangely, Ian Fleming was well-liked at Durnford, the headmaster and owner of the school, Tom Pellatt, taking a fancy to his robust attitude to life. The feeling was not reciprocated, as he quickly managed to tell his mother:

> I am afraid that I do not like school very much. I do not know what form I am in, I'm in so many. I am afraid I have not made many friends; they are so dirty and unrevenant (sic)[1]

The one thing that Durnford did for him was to introduce him to the enjoyment that could be gained from reading and listening to stories being expertly read. Every Sunday evening Pellatt's wife would hold court in her living room where, with her feet being massaged by one of the more favoured pupils, she would read to the boys. It was Mrs Pellatt who introduced Fleming to the adventures of Bulldog Drummond and there were those who would argue that he never progressed much beyond Sapper's lurid prose – a slightly harsh judgement, I think.

In fact, his literary interests at this time were both wide and eclectic. Fleming's saving grace was that those Sunday evenings at Prep School saw him eagerly devour all types and styles of writing. John Buchan, particularly the Hannay stories, quickly became a favourite. Robert Louis Stevenson, Jules Verne and Edgar Allen Poe were close behind. And yet none of them ever really challenged Sapper for Pole Position and the creator of Bulldog Drummond remained a fixture in Fleming's literary imagination for the rest of his life.

Ian and his brother Peter had already begun their time at Durnford when news of their father's death was relayed to the family. The boys were at home, enjoying their Easter holiday – Peter, actually, in hospital having his tonsils removed. They were given little time to grieve but packed off back to Durnford where Mrs Pellatt and her needy feet gave them what comfort she could.

After that the traditional upper-class destination of Eton beckoned for all the boys of the Fleming family. Peter went first and quickly gained a magical and mercurial reputation for himself, excelling at everything to which he turned his hand.

Ian, when his time came, found that it was almost impossible to follow in the footsteps of his gifted elder brother. His solution to the problem was quite simple – he simply stopped trying to compete or keep up, academically at least.

His lack of interest in studying infuriated his housemaster, E V Slater, who saw him as something of a wastrel. He deplored Fleming Minor's personal predilections such as overuse of expensive hair cream, his obsessive interest in his own physical appearance – and the subsequent seemingly all-pervasive attraction to girls.

Where Fleming did succeed in outclassing his elder brother, however, was in sport. Not for him the team games of soccer, rugby, the Wall Game and other favourite Eton sports. He chose athletics, a wide range of sporting activities where the emphasis was on individual effort and achievement. At events like the 400 and 200, discus and long jump he made sure that he was as unbeatable on the athletics track as Peter was in the classroom.

Inevitably, as a skilled athlete, he still played soccer for his House, breaking his nose in a collision with the brother of future Prime Minister Alec Douglas-Home. In his mother's opinion, it spoiled his good looks but Fleming was astute enough to realise that the broken nose gave him something of a piratical appearance which he would exploit for the rest of his life.

He was constantly at war with his Housemaster and found himself being regularly beaten for one misdemeanour or another. Matters became even more explosive when Fleming acquired an old car for which, against all the school regulations, he found garage facilities in the area where the machine could be stored. He would use the car for jaunts around the area and illicit trips into London whenever he could find the time and opportunity to be away from school for a brief respite.

Meanwhile, he continued to excel on the athletics track. In 1924 he won every single event in the Junior Sports Day and soon went on to even greater local glory:

> As a senior he set another record by becoming the only boy in living memory to have been Victor Ludorum (for) two years in succession ... Fleming proved to be the best athlete, one of style, strength and power, that Eton had seen for generations.[2]

Apart from athletics, Ian Fleming had not distinguished himself at school. As a result, E V Slater persuaded his mother that university was not an option and that the army might give her wayward son the discipline he seemed to require.

After a brief period in Eton's Army Class, traditionally the lowest of all the school gradings, he left school for a 'crammer' at Newport Pagnell with a view to working towards passing the examination for Sandhurst College.

***

Surprisingly, Ian Fleming worked hard at his Newport Pagnell crammer. Discipline was relaxed, certainly not 'in his face', and if nothing else the extra freedom and access to girls in the town suited him admirably. It meant that there was little to rebel about and, in due course, he took the Sandhurst exam and astonished everyone – himself more than anyone – by coming sixth in the whole country. It was, however, a false dawn.

Sandhurst was more bound up with discipline than either of Fleming's schools or his crammer had ever been and as soon as he began his period of basic training, he realised that he had made a terrible mistake. Screaming NCOs on the parade ground, hours spent cleaning and pressing the uniform that he hated to wear? It was not for him and, predictably, he lasted less than a year, resigning his commission before he even got it. According to some reports, the only thing that Cadet Ian Fleming left Sandhurst with was a doss of gonorrhoea!

Fleming never spoke about such a misfortune but, given his lifestyle, catching gonorrhoea was possible, almost an occupational hazard. If he did indeed have 'a dose', as the men about town liked to call it, the problem did not affect him unduly.

The final decision about leaving Sandhurst was only made after he had been discovered climbing back into the college after an illegal trip to London to see a girl he was keen on at the time. It was a trivial offence but it was enough to make up Fleming's mind.

Punishment for the offence would have meant being confined to barracks for the next six months. That, to the irrepressible Fleming, who needed the relief and release of London and seemed desperate to prove himself at every gasp of breath, was a non-event. His reaction was inevitable – resignation and escape coming up, sir!

It was 1927 and Eve Fleming was now beginning to despair about her unmanageable son. For a while, she considered the traditional outlet for all wayward sons of the upper classes – send him off to serve the Empire in some out-of-the-way placement. That and cutting off his quite considerable allowance seemed about all she could do.

But like a pebble that had been skimmed across the water, it was time for another skip and change of direction for Fleming. Before his mother could act, he decided on his future direction and informed her that he would like to try for a position in the Foreign Office. It was a challenging route for anyone to take, let alone someone whose educational career so far had been one of total failure.

To begin with he needed to pass the entrance exam. The Foreign Office examination was probably more demanding than any test devised by Oxford or Cambridge with only a handful of the candidates ever being accepted. Fleming understood the difficulty and one is left with the distinct impression that aiming for the Foreign Office exam was a case of him setting himself up for rejection, getting in his almost inevitable failure before anyone or anything else could bring him to the same disaster.

However, in order to have a chance of passing the examination his command of foreign languages, particularly German and French, needed to be brought up to standard. So, next port of call was a small, privately run school in the Austrian town of Kitzbuhal.

He and his brother Peter had already spent a few months at the school which was a strange mixture of gentleman's club, finishing school and crammer. Both Ian and Peter had enjoyed their time there but that had been twelve or eighteen months before, when Peter was waiting to take up a place at Oxford and Ian was preparing to enter Sandhurst.

The young Ian Fleming viewed the prospect of a year or so in Kitzbuhal with a degree of relief. It was considerably better than being sent off to Australia or some other God-forsaken spot that did not even warrant a dot on the map. And, of course, his allowance would continue.

The owners of the school were Ernan Forbes Dennis, a former British spy, and his novelist wife Phyllis Bottome. Excellent linguists, the Forbes Dennis's were also devotees of the psychiatrist Alfred Adler, a post-Freudian practitioner who had firm ideas about the damage caused to younger siblings by successful older brothers. On the face of it, this seemed to be at the root of all Ian Fleming's problems. The school in Kitzbuhal might well be, the Forbes Dennis's thought, an ideal environment for the young and rootless Fleming to sit, improve his German and take stock of his life.

To begin with, Fleming spent most of his time swimming in the lake at Kitzbuhal and climbing the surrounding mountains.

He could look ahead to the winter when the snow came and the skiing slopes would be open again. When winter did finally come, it was clear that he was going to be a powerful performer on the slopes. It was soon equally clear that his success and pleasure at skiing were due to bravery, strength and foolhardiness rather than any particular skill.

He would take terrible risks, skiing off-piste in forbidden areas and seeming to be courting death at every turn. Once he found himself caught in an avalanche, a mountain of snow burying him up to his shoulders. He escaped with minor cuts and bruises and his reputation as a fearless performer on skis was enhanced yet again.

At this early stage in his Kitzbuhal interlude, academic studies counted for little, sitting way down in his list of priorities. Speaking German every day, however, his command of the language improved greatly. For the moment French took only a 'bit part'.

His dashing good looks and the legends that soon grew around him – this was a young British adventurer who had been disowned by his family and so on – meant that the girls in the village were soon clustering around him whenever he appeared at the Café Reisch in Kitzbuhal. Fleming accepted their adoration with a supercilious snobbery which only increased his appeal even more.

Despite his declared interest in a career with the Foreign Office – which was, at least, a plan for the future – things were not entirely straightforward. When he first returned to their school again the Forbes Dennis's had been astounded, maybe even alarmed, by the change in Ian.

He had always been proud and arrogant, now he had periods when he was deeply depressed, almost wallowing in his misery. He seemed to have become withdrawn from the world, even a little neurotic. He gladly accepted the attention of the Café Reisch girls but that meant very little to him. He had, Forbes Dennis decided, no sense of direction in his life, even though he was still filled with ambition. The prospects were not particularly promising.

As far as Fleming was concerned, he had little to be positive about. Cloak it any way he liked, he had enjoyed a less than successful school career and even the army, which had promised so much, had been a disappointing failure. Worse than that, he had barely given Sandhurst a chance to exert its influence, deciding to fail it before it failed him.

According to the theories of Adler, his was a classic case of someone whose goal of superiority had been crushed by the greater successes of an elder sibling – albeit a much-loved one. Ian would, Ernan Forbes Dennis decided, have to be carefully handled. He would start by letting the mountains and the environment cast their spell.

Whatever success the Forbes Dennis's and their school managed to achieve – and it turned out to be considerable – was as much down to Fleming's time in the mountains away from the rigours of home life as it was to the Adlerian theories of his hosts. Just being away from a powerful mother who, in his opinion, was always judging him, was worth its weight in gold bullion. Nevertheless, the Forbes Dennis's watched him carefully, noted his doings and reported back to his mother who was, after all, paying his fees.

Fleming gradually regained some of his self-confidence, coming to terms with his situation and understanding the problems within his personality. As he did so, work seemed to come fairly easily to him. He was never going to be a natural student but, once given an aim, he could work towards it.

He read widely, particularly writers like Kafka and Rilke, and was an avid fan of Georges Simenon and his main character Inspector Maigret. He brought his German up to an impeccable level, became passably fluent in French and even taught himself to speak and understand Russian.

In the after-dinner soirees with Phyllis Bottome, he and the other students began to write stories, fantasy pieces with their Gothic roots set firmly in the Austrian mountains and lakes. This was an activity which appealed to Ian but, for the time being, literary life was hardly something he thought seriously about.

At the end of his time at the school, however, Ian Fleming was a far more rounded character than he would have been had he continued with his army career. He did not see it at the time but his experiences at Kitzbuhal were to help shape him for life.

It would be wrong to say that Forbes Dennis and his wife had 'cured' Ian Fleming of his doubts and feelings of insecurity. But they did teach him to live with them, to become the best he could ever be – in whatever field of life he went on to choose. The important thing was not to be consumed by his inner worries and concerns. For that Ian Fleming was eternally grateful.

***

Fleming's love of books – as objects in their own right – began during his time at Kitzbuhal. That love would grow and become a passion for him as, over the years, he built up one of the truly great individual libraries in the country, a collection of first editions that was unsurpassed. For the moment, however, there were other matters to be dealt with.

He had spent a year at Kitzbuhal and Forbes Dennis now decided that, with the Foreign Office exam looming, he should go on to Munich to live with a German family and study at the university. It would, he decided, be the final element in Fleming's wider education.

Forbes Dennis was probably right. Fleming enjoyed his time in the Bavarian city, living the wild life of a student, although he rarely attended lectures or seminars. He was, however, a regular in the student bars and cafes where he was accepted almost immediately as simply being a regular member of 'the crowd'.

He even survived a visit from his mother. Early on in his stay in Munich, Eve Fleming descended on the city like a wolf on the fold, checking out everything her son had done and experienced. If Ian was going to continue claiming his allowance, she was going to make damned sure he was worth it. She went away convinced that he was spending his time well – and, indeed, thanks to the relaxed Munich atmosphere his periods of depression had greatly reduced.

Munich was followed by a period in Geneva where Fleming became an external student at Geneva University. His French improved but the Swiss city did not impress him:

> The beautiful lake, plus the highest fountain in the world and the Rhone that thunders so majestically through the town – all this and Mount Blanc too, do not make Geneva a happy town. The spirit of Calvin, expressed in the ugly and uncompromising cathedral that dominates the city seems to brood like a thunderous conscience over the inhabitants.[3]

One thing that he did like about Geneva was a young girl with whom he reportedly fell in love. His affair with Monique Panchaud de Bottens was his first serious relationship but her appeal had far more to do with the freedom he now felt – his mother had agreed to a continuation of his allowance and to the forthcoming attempt at the Foreign Office – than it ever did to any deep or amorous emotions.

The affair managed to survive Fleming's time in Geneva and his return to England. He was not yet ready to settle down into any sort of domesticity, however, and the relationship eventually fizzled out – but not before Monique paid a visit to London where she stayed with Fleming and his mother in the family house in Cheyne Walk.

Eve Fleming was not impressed and told Ian exactly what she felt about the girl. It was enough to put the final nail in the coffin!

He did not write much while in Geneva but he did continue collecting his old first editions and even added to his collection a passport once owned by Benito Mussolini. The 'Fleming Library' was stored away and rarely looked at by Ian. It was a case of possession and knowledge that it actually existed which really mattered to the young man.

He did, however, translate a lecture/paper given by Jung. It was a bizarre and not particularly interesting piece about Paracelsus and, perhaps inevitably, the English translation was never published.

Fleming returned to London in December 1930. The Foreign Office examinations were now looming like one of his beloved Swiss mountains above his head, albeit with considerably more menace. He knew that it was time now to prove to everyone that his extended stay in Kitzbuhal, Munich and Geneva had been well spent.

Just over sixty applicants were examined in 1931, the process taking ten long days and, true to his view of himself, Fleming came up short. He finished in a highly respectable twenty-fifth place out of sixty-two but as only five aspiring diplomats were to be selected for jobs, he was not one of them.

Perhaps his view of the world and, more significantly, his way of expressing it were not what the Foreign Office wanted. His English paper was his poorest result, garnering him just twenty marks out of a hundred. That, viewed now with hindsight, seems to have been a bizarre result – obviously the world was not yet ready for the literary style of Ian Fleming.

Suddenly all the freedom and joy that he had carefully built up during his time in Switzerland and Germany came crashing down around Fleming's shoulders. He had failed yet again and was at a loss about where he should go from here. He did not know it but a whole new chapter of life experiences was about to open up before him.

Chapter Six

A Good War

Ian Fleming was devastated by his failure to gain a place in the Foreign Office. It was a failure that had come about despite considerable hard work and effort and it infuriated him. He felt humiliated and rejected, so much so that ever afterwards he lied about his final position in the exam gradings. Seventh, he told everyone, he had finished in seventh place. It certainly sounded better than twenty-fifth!

The possibility of a career in the Foreign Office behind him, Fleming endured the agony of a few months under his mother's roof, all the while being reminded by her of yet another failure to be listed on his CV. Ian's failure seemed to have hurt her as much as it had done him. Eve was like a dog with a bone, quarrel after quarrel making life hard for both of them.

And then – respite. Out of the blue, he was offered a job at the Reuters News Agency, a six months trial on a more than substantial wage. Whether or not Eve Fleming had 'pulled strings' to get him the job remains unclear but, regardless of that, Ian was delighted. Six months became twelve and he spent the time as a sub-editor in Reuters newsroom in London, making occasional trips out to various venues and locations when offered a reporting opportunity.

Fleming clearly impressed the Reuters managers and, in April 1933, he was given the opportunity of a lifetime. Many of the Reuter's newshounds would have leapt at the chance he was now given but it was offered to Fleming and he knew a golden opportunity when he saw one.

In the Soviet Union, six British engineers had been accused of espionage and arrested. Stalin's State Trials, his infamous purges, were just beginning but the arrest of foreign workers was unusual and, therefore, of national and international interest.

That spring, much to his surprise and enjoyment, Ian Fleming found himself ensconced in a sleeping compartment on the Nord Express from Berlin, steaming through northern Germany on a train that was second only to the famous Orient Express for romance and comfort. There were no secret agents lurking in the corridors or at the bar, at least as far as he could tell, but Ian Fleming was bound for Moscow to cover the trials. And anything was possible in the weeks ahead.

In Moscow, he stayed at the National Hotel, along with all of the other journalists and reporters who were covering the story. He was young and inexperienced but he learned quickly from the old hands who frequented the American Bar in the hotel. Men like the American Walter Duranty and *the Daily Telegraph's* A T Cholerton became lasting friends.

At one stage Fleming applied for a personal interview with Joseph Stalin. He didn't get it but he did receive a signed note from the Russian leader expressing regret for his inability to grant an interview and offering pressure of work as an excuse for the failure.

Fleming's trip was hugely successful. He expertly supplied regular copy for Reuters, making much out of the rumour machine that was in operation in Moscow. His articles were light and were always well received, both by Reuters and by the newspapers that printed his material.

The trial itself lasted seven days and was a classic example of a police state at work. Fleming reported on the inevitable series of convictions – although the sentences were all somewhat more lenient than anyone expected.

More importantly, he stored away the images and memories of the Russian judges and officials, men like Vassili Ulrich, who was something of a classic Fleming villain. The memories were ready for use at some stage in the future. He did not know when or how they would be used but they never left him. It took twenty-five years for his memory bank and imagination to click into place but when they did, he was able to produce incredibly realistic cameos and set scenes for what was probably his masterpiece, *From Russia with Love*. It was all courtesy of that pre-war Reuters trip to Moscow.

As the trials progressed, Fleming contrived several complicated and clever ways of getting his news back to Reuters before anyone else. He even went so far as to damage all of the public phones outside the courtroom save one, which only he knew about and could locate. It was a cross between schoolboy hijinks and professional 'stop at nothing' tactics.

In the end, however, when the guilty verdicts were handed down, he was beaten to the punch by Sergei Mikhailov of Central News Agency, whose reports were published first. It hardly mattered. Fleming's copy was superbly written and when he returned to London, he was offered the much sought-after post of Far Eastern correspondent for Reuters.

To everyone's amazement, he turned down the offer. The death of his grandfather Robert Fleming that same year had brought Ian no financial reward but it did suddenly force on him the idea that he could make a lot more money from banking than he ever could from journalism. And making money was always crucially important for Ian Fleming.

He duly spent the next six years working in banking and stock broking. He began with the firm of Cull and Co, before moving on to Rowe and Pitman where he soon became a junior partner.

Just as he had become a reporter for Reuters without any journalistic experience, so Ian Fleming now moved easily into the world of high finance with even less credibility or specific knowledge. It hardly mattered. He had bravado and a copious amount of cheek and they certainly got him through. He also had his family connections to the firm of Robert Fleming and that was probably the most significant advantage he could find.

Despite lack of experience and knowledge, he did reasonably well, albeit without being as hugely successful as he had hoped. The fortune he had hoped to accumulate did not materialise. Emotionally and practically, he quickly realised, he was not suited to the world of banking:

> He had found himself a comfortable niche at Rowe and Pitman, where one of his regular jobs was writing up the monthly news-sheet ... The big money he had been hoping for never materialized, and it was soon clear that he lacked entirely the right temperament and ability.[1]

Fleming earned enough money to establish and then keep up an extravagant lifestyle and to add to his growing collection of First Editions. He employed a book dealer to hunt down copies of rare books, subject and author irrelevant. All that mattered was the rarity of the book and its likelihood to increase in value.

Within his clique, his wide selection of friends and acquaintants, he was soon renowned as something of a gambler and rake. He became a regular at the casino tables of London and, perhaps more significantly, a philanderer of great note.

He loved to be in the presence of women but he did not really care about or for them. Love was totally out of the question. Unlike most of the men in tradition-bound Britain, he had no shame or reservations about sex. Women were there for his pleasure, he believed; they knew what they were going to get if they became involved with him. It was selfish and supremely uncaring but it was an attitude that was to remain with him until the end.

He had quickly realised that the business of making money through banking and through the buying and selling of stocks and shares was financially productive but it was also something that actually bored him to death. Even so, he endured it – after all, there was little else that he could do without taking a major gamble or risk. And, long before, Ian Fleming had learned his lesson at the gambling table – only bet on certainties.

When he cared to think about it, Fleming's life was one torpid mess of a job he did not like, women who he used and then disowned and a routine that was mind-blowingly stultifying. The trouble was, he liked money and his job, while hardly making him a millionaire, did at least give him a good standard of living.

In the end, Ian Fleming was saved from his boring existence, not by his own desires but by the machinations of Adolph Hitler and the Nazis! However, that lay in the future. Before that, he had an unexpected return to Russia to occupy his mind.

***

Fleming certainly needed something to take his mind off the terminally boring business of buying and selling stocks and shares. For many people, his lifestyle was a thing of envy. Not for Ian Fleming. He had woven a web of ease around himself but that was something which, with typical self-destructive ease, he was constantly trying to rip apart.

He had found himself a house in London, a strange place in Ebury Street that looked more like an old chapel than a terraced house. Sir Oswald Mosley, leader of the British Union of Fascists, had lived there for a while and at some stage, the house had been both a school and a nightclub. Fleming re-designed the interior to his own tastes and established a routine where his friends would come to dine and play bridge two or three times a week. At the weekends they would play golf together.

It all filled Fleming's days and nights but it was an empty existence and the more he lived the life, the more boring and mindless it became. And when he looked around him the more obvious that became.

His brother Peter had written two superb travel books about his jaunts to way-out places with the result that, in the face of Peter's success, even the possibility of writing seemed to have eluded him. When he returned from school on the Continent, Ian might have had ideas about putting pen to paper, particularly when his journalistic articles seemed to be so well appreciated. His brother's two books had effectively stymied that. He had no intention of putting himself up against Peter for comparison and, as he saw it, inevitable failure.

So, when, on the strength of his previous work for Reuters and his more than valuable reports on the country, he was asked to go back to the USSR Ian Fleming leapt at the chance. Reuters had been his one major success in life and this was a second opportunity that he could not refuse. Apart from anything else the job was not as simple or as straightforward as it seemed. There were to be wheels within wheels.

Fleming was officially part of a Trade Mission to Moscow, representing *The Times* newspaper. Unofficially, however, he would be working for the Foreign Office, his brief being to report back to British Intelligence on the strength and readiness of Russian military forces.

His visit to Moscow lasted just five days, most of which he spent showing off to other journalists, trying to impress them by his guise as an 'old Moscow hand'. The trip was largely a waste of time but Fleming used his skills with the written word to provide a more than adequate report which admirably summed up the Russian character:

> But when the moment comes for action, they (the enemy) will realise that these tough grey-faced little men (the average height of the army is 5'5") they are a vastly different force from the ill-equipped gun fodder of 1914.[2]

Once back in London with his report written and delivered to the Foreign Office, Fleming prepared to pick up his old routines. He did not realise that, with war looming, Rear Admiral John Godfrey, Director of Naval Intelligence, had already earmarked him as exactly

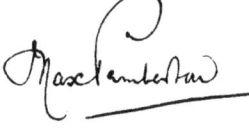

Above left: Max Pemberton, one of the most successful early spy novelists

Above right: The cover of a collection of short stories by Pemberton, suitably gaudy and compelling

Right: William Le Queux, perhaps the most celebrated early spy novelist

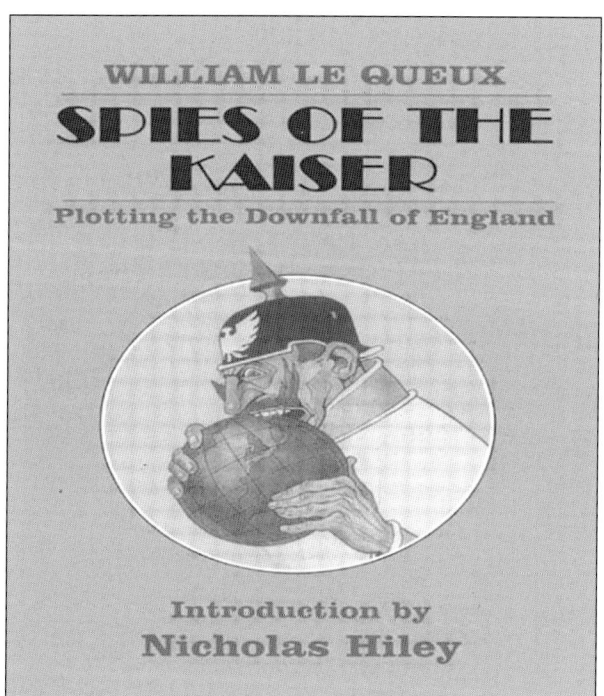

Left: The cover of *Spies of the Kaiser* by Le Queux

Below: Erskine Childers, the photograph taken when he was serving in the British Yeomanry during the Boer War

Erskine Childers and his wife on board their yacht, a somewhat poignant photograph considering his book *The Riddle of the Sands* and his eventual fate

Above left: John Buchan, author of *The Thirty-Nine Steps*

Above right: Buchan was, for a long while, one of the most renowned authors in the world – he even made it onto the cover of *Time* magazine

The cover of *Greenmantle*, possibly Buchan's best book

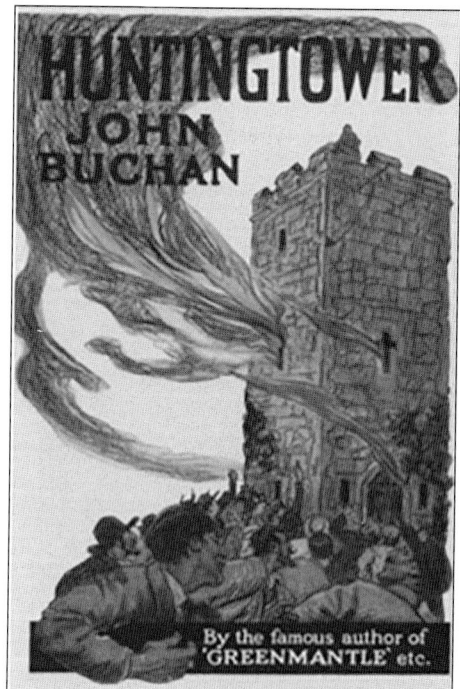

The first edition cover of Buchan's *Huntingtower*

Right: Alfred Hitchcock, Director of the first *Thirty-Nine Steps* film

Below: Hannay on the run, an image from the Kenneth Moore version of The Thirty-Nine Steps

John Buchan in uniform during the First World War

Film poster for *The Thirty-Nine Steps*

Above: The Forth Bridge which never featured in the book *The Thirty-Nine Steps* but played a significant part in Hitchcock's film and other adaptations

Right: Poster announcing a public lecture by Buchan

Robert Donat and Madeline Carroll, the two stars of the first Buchan/Hitchcock film

Buchan is installed as Governor General of Canada

John Buchan replete in traditional native American headgear

Ian Fleming, creator of the best-known spy in the world

The cover of Fleming's *Goldfinger*, probably his most popular book although not necessarily his best

The Old Admiralty building in London where Fleming spent most of the war years

The quad at Eton College – associations with both Fleming and John le Carre

Ian Fleming on the beach below Goldeneye in Jamaica

The Cold War caught and held the interest of the public. Incidents like the Cuban Missile Crisis ensured the success of the Bond books. This shows a Russian cargo boat, carrying missiles, being shadowed by a Neptune aircraft of the USA

Sean Connery, surely the ultimate James Bond

Hoagy Carmichael, the American actor and possible model for the raffish Bond

David Cornwell, aka John le Carre, in his later years

Left: The cover design for *Smiley's People*

Below left: Apart from Cornwell/le Carre the sleepy West German town of Bonn had only one famous resident – Ludwig Beethoven

Below right: Alec Guinness, circa 1972, when his interpretation of George Smiley was all the rage

The opening image of *Tinker Tailor Soldier Spy*, the hit TV series

Winter snow in Kitzbuhal

Above: The grave of John Buchan

Left: Ian Fleming's memorial

the type of man he needed to assist him in his duties. The old routine had gone forever.

Fleming and Godfrey met for the first time in the Carlton Grill – nothing if not classic Fleming territory – one May morning just a few weeks after Ian had returned from Moscow. Godfrey had spent some time hunting for a man who could act as his personal assistant and aid him in his intelligence-gathering duties.

Godfrey's First World War counterpart, Admiral Reginald 'Blinker' Hall, had used a stockbroker as his personal assistant and Godfrey saw no reason not to follow suit. He had Fleming investigated, liked what he found and set up the meeting.

The meeting went well and the offer of a job came a few days later. Fleming accepted with alacrity and began a gradual integration process. He spent the next three months working on the stock market in the mornings and every afternoon for Godfrey in Room 39 at the Admiralty.

When war was declared in September 1939, he became a full-time member of Godfrey's staff, initially with the rank of Lieutenant. He was soon promoted to Lieutenant Commander and eventually rose to be Commander – exactly the same rank as his famous creation James Bond.

As the personal assistant to Admiral Godfrey, Ian Fleming was essentially a 'desk jockey', a man who enjoyed what he and others would later call a 'good war'. Even so, he was always eager to get away from Whitehall to engage in a little active service.

He was in France when that country fell to the Germans in 1940, ostensibly with the aim of convincing Admiral Darlan, commander of the French Navy, to bring his valuable battleships to England where they would supplement the ships of the Royal Navy. It was a hopeless task. Darlan prevaricated, the French ships remained in their ports and Fleming actually spent most of his time organising the evacuation of VIPs from Bordeaux.

Through bluff and the easy exercise of his authority, Ian Fleming performed a valuable service in the face of disaster and danger.

As well as arranging for the transportation of many valuable documents which would otherwise have fallen into Nazi hands, he also facilitated the evacuation of hundreds of displaced Britishers – along with the family of King Zog of Albania!

Fleming was one of the last men to leave Bordeaux, sailing with the British Ambassador on board the cruiser HMS *Arethusa*. He had thoroughly enjoyed his time in France, shrugging off the dangers from bombs and machine gun bullets. Now it was back to the desk in Room 39 in the Admiralty.

Over the next few years, he proved to be a great compiler of would-be or potential operations. One of his suggestions involved the capture of a fast German motor launch. Dozens of the German launches, E-Boats as they became known, were operating along the French coast and the Royal Navy was eager to lay hands on one. Unfortunately, his idea came to nothing due to the lack of a captured, working enemy flying boat, something which was an essential element of the plan.

As the war progressed Fleming came up with several more plots and plans. Many of these were quite fantastic but all of them showed his fertile imagination at work.

In June 1941 he accompanied Admiral Godfrey on a top-secret mission to Washington to court J Edgar Hoover and the FBI and to gain their support for Britain in what was then a lone stand against Nazi Germany. The trip involved a stopover in Lisbon, waiting for the Clipper flying boat which would take the pair to America.

Fleming later claimed that he had spent the whole of one evening during the wait playing baccarat against Nazi agents. It was, he said, his patriotic duty to relieve the Nazis of their cash, but the story was just that, a story, a fantasy or a made-up tale, another of his imaginative flights of fancy.

During the visit, he did play a long and physically draining game of baccarat but only against Portuguese gamblers, not Nazi spies, and lost all of his money in the process. He stored away the facts of the affair, developing and enlarging them in the process, and his imagination again came into play when he recreated the event in *Casino Royale,* his first Bond novel.

During this trip to America Fleming became friendly with the former Presidential aide and soon-to-be head of the American secret service 'Wild Bill' Donovan. He helped Donovan in the writing of the charter that eventually created America's CIA. It was all important stuff and Ian Fleming revelled in every minute of it.

During his time working for Admiral Godfrey, the rapacious Fleming became fascinated with the gadgets that the spies with whom he was constantly rubbing shoulders used in their work. He fell in love with a flat-bladed commando throwing knife, obtained one for himself and took it with him wherever he went. Other 'inventions', like a fountain pen which fired gas, were to occupy another role in his life to come.

One of Fleming's major contributions to the war effort was to take charge of Operation Goldeneye. This was a proposed plan to establish and maintain an intelligence network in Spain, to be put into operation should the Nazis ever make a move into General Franco's fascist state.

Gibraltar was to be the centre for British sabotage operations but in the end, Hitler did not invade Spain and, like so many of Fleming's wartime adventures, Operation Goldeneye came to nothing. The idea was dropped but the name caught Fleming's imagination and was to live on – in a different country, in what was really a very different world.

Fleming was involved in producing – possibly even writing – what was referred to as The Trout Memo. This was a document outlining the importance of deceiving the enemy in wartime, hence the seeming irrelevance and reference to fish in the title. One of the suggestions in the document was the planting of a corpse carrying false papers, a plan that was later used, under the heading of Operation Mincemeat, to mislead German defenders about the invasion of Sicily in 1943.

Heavily involved in the 'secret war', Ian Fleming managed to retain facts and information that he would later use in his Bond novels. One impressive Nazi who later found his way into one of Fleming's books was Otto Skorzeny, the rescuer of Mussolini from his mountain top imprisonment after the Italian dictator was deposed and held captive.

Fleming had already been mightily impressed by Skorzeny's handling of his small team of guerrillas and commandoes during the German invasion of Crete, long before the Mussolini episode. The rescue of the Italian leader from his seemingly impregnable prison simply added to Fleming's admiration.

As a result, when the opportunity came, he developed his own assault group, Number 30 Assault Unit, based on the same lines as Skorzeny's team. Fleming was not finished with Skorzeny. The bull-necked German had made a great impression on him and achieved literary immortality as Hugo Drax in the third Bond novel *Moonraker*.

Number 30 Assault Unit quickly became Fleming's pride and joy. He loved working with, and for, what he dubbed his little 'band of Red Indians'.

They were a small group of commando warriors, initially just thirty strong but eventually rising to over a hundred hard and driven men, willing and able to carry out hazardous operations. Fleming chose them and trained them himself, then sent them out on their perilous missions. He was not allowed to go himself, Admiral Godfrey declaring that he was too valuable to risk.

Fleming's Red Indians were active in North Africa, Italy and several other theatres of war before, at the end of 1942, he lost his mentor. Admiral Godfrey moved on to become Flag Officer, Royal Indian Navy and was replaced by Rear Admiral Edward Rushbrake, a man with more traditional views on the role of his personal assistant. As a result, in the second part of his war Fleming became increasingly more desk-bound.

Fleming was not exactly happy to relinquish direct command of Number 30 Assault Unit but he had become somewhat estranged from the team. Many did not like his referring to them as a 'Band of Red Indians', feeling that it demeaned their contribution to the war.

As far as Fleming was concerned his work with the commandoes had been good while it lasted. Now there were other things on his mind.

At about the same time as Godfrey moved on, Fleming suffered a personal loss when a long-time girlfriend – albeit a much abused and mistreated girlfriend – was killed in a bombing raid. She had been working as a motorcycle despatch rider and one of the last things she did for Fleming was to go out of her way to pick up 200 cigarettes from his supplier.

Fleming ploughed on regardless, developing a training course for potential members of his commando group. The regime and what can be loosely described as the curriculum for the training course were based on an intensive training regime planned and run by Wild Bill Donovan and by Canadian spy runner Bill Stephenson.

This American training base was actually in Canada, just over the border from the USA at Oshawa, close to Toronto, where Fleming himself, during visits to America, had endured many of the tricks and tasks of what had then become the OSS.

It would have been easy for Fleming to simply sit on the sidelines and watch what Donovan and his trainers were doing. That was not his style. He wanted to participate with the result that neither Fleming nor his tutors held anything back. He was, by all accounts, one of the top trainees, although he did quail at carrying out the final task, actually killing a man, face to face.

Fleming was peripherally involved in the breaking of the Enigma Code but was more instrumental in creating T-Force. This was another special unit whose purpose was to capture and then shield important enemy documents and, if necessary, people as well.

As the war entered its final phase documentation and plans of the German V2 rockets became vitally important and Fleming was with his new guerrillas in T-Force as they closed in on the rocket bases in the Low Countries. It was too good a chance to miss and, as he knew, the war was ending. Such opportunities might never come again.

Never one to waste or forget potential material, much of the information and material gathered from this raid was later to form an essential component of his novel *Moonraker*.

The war in Europe ended in May 1945, the Far Eastern conflict concluding a few months later. Ian Fleming had few illusions or regrets about what had been and would now be no more. To use an old-fashioned and well-used cliché, the war had been a good one for him. Now it was over. He was discharged from the Navy in November 1945.

He had two weeks paid leave in which to consider his future and one thing was abundantly clear. He was not going to go back to 'the city', to his pre-war job in banking and stock broking. He was not yet ready to earn a living from his pen but he was close, very close indeed.

Chapter Seven

Bond, Alive and Kicking

Long before the end of the war, Ian Fleming had made two important decisions that would have a profound effect on his life. Firstly, he would abandon Britain and live abroad and, secondly, he would write the greatest spy novel in the world.

The first of these decisions was easy to set in motion – in theory, at least. At the end of 1944, he and an old friend named Ivar Bryce attended a three-day conference in Jamaica. Fleming fell in love with the island, paid £2,000 for a plot of land on the north coast – bought sight unseen – and decided to build a house overlooking Rum Bay. The house was an austere, simple place but it suited Fleming perfectly and he gleefully named it Goldeneye.

There was, however, something of a problem. Fleming had grown used to wielding considerable power and, thanks to his time in Room 39, had come to enjoy the wheeling and dealing that accompanied his position as the second most important man in Naval Intelligence. As much as he enjoyed fishing and water sports, the idea of spending the rest of his days lying idly in the sun began to pall long before the building work on Goldeneye was even completed.

The second aim was even more difficult to achieve. Writing a novel was not as easy as he had made out. Inspiration and discipline were essential ingredients and, despite his grandiose claims, Fleming was still faced with a considerable degree of self-doubt. The proposed novel was, for the moment, placed on the back burner.

Instead, he accepted an offer of work from newspaper magnate Lord Kemsley who wanted him to create a Foreign News Service for his chain of national and regional papers. The starting salary would be £5,000 per annum. Written into Fleming's contract was the specific clause that he would be entitled to a block of two months' holiday each year. This period, he told himself, he would spend at his new house in Jamaica.

Fleming immediately established a regular routine, just as he had done before the war. This time, however, it would be far more fulfilling. He would work at building up Kemsley's Foreign News Agency for ten months of the year, dining at his favourite restaurants and courting those people who would be useful to him. He would travel to important locations in order to build and develop his networks. Then he would head off for two months in his version of paradise.

During his years working for the Kemsley papers, particularly on *The Sunday Times*, he developed his persona even down to the clothes he invariably wore each day – a polka dot blue bow tie, moccasin shoes and dark blue suit. His Morland's Specials, up to 70 or 80 a day, were now smoked from an elegant cigarette holder. It was all acting out a part but it sustained him through the dark November and December days until it was time to return, once more, to Jamaica.

Goldeneye was basic in the extreme, as guests soon discovered. Fleming's first stay in January 1946 set the pattern, taking place before building work on the house was even half completed. It mattered not. Food pulled from the sea, homemade furniture set on garishly decorated concrete floors, a wide range of his own unusual but potent cocktails – Fleming was in his element. Actor and writer Noël Coward was a near neighbour and, with the same sense of humour and view of life, the two men became the best of friends.

With a shallow reef just off-shore, Fleming and his guests were regular snorkelers, watching life on the reef and catching crayfish for dinner. Guests were many and varied, ranging from the writer Truman Capote to Noël Coward who had full use of the house while his own property was being renovated. Politician Anthony Eden also came to relax and recuperate during his final illness.

Fleming enjoyed courting danger. He had done it for years on the ski slopes of Europe. Now the Caribbean would offer him opportunities to push his courage and resolve even more.

The peculiar, not to say potentially, lethal game of lassoing sharks soon became a regular pastime. Fleming was ably assisted in the pastime by his Jamaican friend and professional fisherman Aubyn Cousins. Cousins was the original for Quarrel, Bond's Cayman Island companion who appeared as a 'supporting act' in both *Live and Let Die* and *Dr No*.

He might kill off Quarrel in *Dr No* but Aubyn Cousins remained a firm comrade for the rest of Fleming's life. Interestingly, Fleming would never allow Cousins to kill a shark during their lassoing expeditions. Once the excitement and the fear of being overturned by the thrashing creature had evaporated it was time to set it free to return to the deep:

> The reef was simply a place of escape. By the mere act of donning flippers and mask he was back in the sort of world Captain Nemo inhabited in the Jules Verne books he read as a child ... a world where boredom vanishes, where loneliness no longer matters.[1]

Once again, Fleming was play-acting, filling the role others expected of him. And when the Bond books began to be successful, he was simply living the life that the creator of 007 just *had* to enjoy – as every reader knew!

By the beginning of the 1950s, Fleming's own life had become rather confused. For several years he had been involved in an intense and lasting affair with Ann Charteris whose husband had been killed in the war. On his death, she had expected Fleming to propose. It did not happen and she married Viscount Rothermere – while still continuing her affair with Fleming. In 1948 Ann gave birth to Fleming's daughter but the baby was stillborn.

Viscount Rothermere divorced Ann Charteris in 1952, citing Fleming as one of the principal causes of the marriage breakdown. Feeling, perhaps, that it was now time to settle down, Ian Fleming finally married Ann in Jamaica on 24 March 1952. Their son Caspar was born just a few months later.

The marriage was a tempestuous affair, both Ian and Ann indulging in extra-marital affairs, Ann with Hugh Gaitskell and Ian with his Jamaican neighbour Blanche Blackwell, mother of one of the founders of the Reggae music outlet, Island Records. As many of his friends, not to mention his enemies, might have said, nothing changes!

Change, however, was certainly on the cards as far as Fleming was concerned. By the early fifties Fleming, like most of the journalists and reporters in the Kemsley empire, was feeling considerable pressure from television and radio. TV, in particular, could obtain and circulate news far quicker than old-fashioned print sources could ever dream possible and the role of newspapers was having to change. Many of the old hacks were unable and unwilling to change with them. The new slant, away from news breaking towards leisure and social interest certainly had little appeal for Fleming.

Fleming's position as Foreign Manager was increasingly under threat, a situation made worse by the fact that certain elements within the Kemsley empire were determined to get rid of this posing dilettante who had the luxury of spending two months in the Caribbean every year. Fleming could almost feel the knives hovering close to his back.

Inevitably, he took everything personally and he was soon deep in depression. He had not been well for some time but he ignored doctor's advice to cut down on the cigarettes and alcohol. He had trouble with stones in his kidneys, one attack frightening him particularly badly. Already doctors were warning him that the possibility of a heart attack was not far away.

He battled on, more afraid of failure than ever. He helped his mother when she chose to move to Cable Beach at Nassau in the Bahamas but the taxation problems that had prompted her move now also began to affect him. Life in post-war Britain was not easy for the rich or semi-rich and Fleming's lifestyle was under significant pressure.

In an effort to raise the money he began to regularly rent out Goldeneye, even charging his friend Noël Coward £50 a week for an extended stay at the house. In late 1950 he seriously considered selling off his library of first editions but in the end, he could not bear to part with the collection and so the idea came to nothing. Ian Fleming was fortunate – he had another avenue to try before realising his assets.

***

Many writers produce their best work when they are under pressure or strain. The concentrated effort required to come up with quality content, be it a piece of fiction, a book of factual writing or a volume of poetry, has always demanded heightened awareness and a brain sharpened almost to the point of self-destruction. And that was exactly the case with Ian Fleming.

He had prevaricated for years, putting off the moment of creation time and time again. But now, with financial difficulties and the very real possibility of yet another failure looming in front of him, he began to finally write his long-threatened first novel. He later claimed that one of the motives for writing this first book was to distract him from concern about his forthcoming marriage. There might well be an element of truth in that 'throw away' comment.

Over the years he had built up a huge reservoir of facts and detailed information about the world of espionage, along with a whole range of atmospheric impressions. Characters like the Russian judges he encountered during his time in Moscow and the inimitable Otto Skorzeny were hovering, waiting to be brought into reality. By the early 1950s, this pool of knowledge was still largely untapped but, at the same time, it was never far from the forefront of his brain.

Fleming would probably not have appreciated the analogy but these facts and memories were the emotional and literary equivalent of the 'sleepers' and 'moles' buried deep in western society by enemy agents and spies – at least in the fictional world created by men like John le Carré and John Buchan.

As was abundantly clear, such characters did not just exist in fiction, there were many real-life examples. They were moles who could lie hidden for years; Kim Philby and the rest of the Cambridge Five had proved that. And that was how it was with Fleming's personal store of knowledge.

Facts, experiences, characters – they were all there to tap into whenever he was finally ready. During the war years and in the immediate aftermath of conflict Fleming had been besieged with other things to keep him busy. He had not been in the right frame of mind with his self-doubt always too dominant. Now he was driven to write.

Fear of poverty was very real for Ian Fleming but it was not just a way of making money that unleashed him onto his typewriter. More importantly, writing this first book was a means of dealing with the worries and concerns that were rushing toward him like a tsunami.

Fleming wrote the book in two months, beginning on 17 February 1952. He wrote it on a battered old typewriter at Goldeneye, 2,000 words a day, making alterations and amendments in pencil on the manuscript and transporting it back to London when his 'holiday' finished. In London, the MS was properly and professionally typed by his secretary – who became, incidentally, the inspiration for Miss Moneypenny, M's feisty guardian and doorkeeper. Only after the success of *Casino Royale* did Fleming allow himself the luxury of a new typewriter, in his case a gold-plated machine on which all future Bond stories were typed.

Casino Royale remains one of Fleming's greatest achievements. It is a book which has, perhaps, the most effective opening and closing lines in any piece of espionage fiction. In that, if not in content, the comparison with Charles Dickens's *A Tale of Two Cities* is unavoidable:

> The scent and smoke and sweat of a casino are nauseating at three in the morning. Then the soul-erosion produced from high gambling – a compost of greed and fear and nervous tension – becomes unbearable and the senses awake and revolt from it.[2]

The picture Fleming paints in this opening paragraph is memorable, compelling and revolting at the same time. Repeated use of the conjunction 'and' gives the writing a sense of urgency, giving to the scene an emotion that belies the atmosphere of the half-awake casino and its gamblers – 'the scent and smoke and sweat', 'greed and fear and nervous tension' and so on.

It was an enchanting and even romantic beginning for any novel. To the physically and emotionally drained populace of post-war Britain that was crucially important. In 1952, when he was writing his book, meat and petrol were still rationed in the war-damaged country, foreign travel was a distant luxury and the idea of gambling for high stakes merely a dream:

> Most British households did not have a car, a telephone or a television. Many cities, especially London and the ports were still cratered with bomb-sites, crumbling buildings and rampant willowherb.[3]

This was very far from the picture that *Casino Royale* provided for its readers. Fleming was creating a world that, in 1953 and '54 was about as far removed from the experience of most people as the dark side of the moon. What he offered his readers was a world of expensive restaurants and fine food, giving them a taste of fast cars and exotic locations. His writing was so vivid and so real that those readers believed him implicitly. And they longed to experience it, if only through the fictional activities of James Bond. Small wonder, then, that the book was in its third edition within a month of publication.

If the opening paragraph of *Casino Royale* set a scene of hope and desire, the concluding words show the brutality of his hero's world:

> He spoke quietly into the receiver.
>
> "This is 007 speaking. This is an open line. It's an emergency. Can you hear me? Pass this on at once. 3030 was a double, working for Redland."
>
> "Yes, dammit, I said 'was.' The bitch is dead now."[4]

That was how people spoke. It was *not* how they wrote. But Fleming's clipped sentences – no literary pretensions, deliberately short and to the point – give his writing an urgency and a sense of shock that is vital to the ending and to the success of the whole story.

As with Buchan before him, and Erskine Childers before that, Fleming made sure that *Casino Royale* was filled with descriptive detail. The clothes that Bond and Vesper wear, the restaurants they frequent, the streets through which they parade, it is all offered to the reader in fascinating detail. The organisation of SMERSH, the Russian anti-spy agency believed by the British to be under the direct control of Lavrentiy Beria, is outlined in considerable detail. None of it allows the pace of the novel to slow or flag; it is, in fact, as compelling as the central storyline.

This is particularly true with the scenes describing the gambling duel between Bond and the villain Le Chiffre. Lifted directly from Fleming's own memory of his night at the gambling table in Lisbon back in 1942, it is compelling writing. Most of Fleming's readers would never have played baccarat and would never do so at any stage in the future. Fleming's skill is that he shows his audience how the game is played while never once losing the impetus of the story.

When viewed objectively it is clear that *Casino Royale* is an unusual and very different type of espionage thriller. Bulldog Drummond, this is not! Fleming's hero loses throughout the story, enduring failure after failure in his attempt to bring down the villain.

He loses his stake at cards and is only saved by the assistance of CIA agent Felix Leiter. Then he is at the mercy of Le Chiffre, naked and afraid, but is again saved, this time by the intervention of a SMERSH agent – who leaves him with a message or monogram carved onto the back of his hand. And eventually he loses out with Vesper Lynd, who is revealed as a double agent. And so on. He wins, ultimately, by luck rather than by any specific wielding of skill or good judgement.

If the villain of the piece is perhaps not up to the later standard of enemies like Mr Big, Goldfinger, Red Grant, Rosa Klebb and Blofeld, there are compensations. In *Casino Royale*, Fleming begins the pattern which continues for virtually all of his spy novels – Bond suffers torture, both physical and emotional, which he endures, emerging successful at the end.

One of the criticisms of Fleming's writing is that as the series of Bond books progressed, he became more and more enamoured with violence. Perhaps so, but there is no doubt that the famous torture scene in *Casino Royale* where Le Chiffre tries to emasculate Bond with a carpet beater is not exactly a soft option with which to begin.

Before Fleming presented his manuscript to Jonathan Cape in 1952, he had been given 'the thumbs up' by his friend, the poet/novelist William Plomer. His brother Peter had also expressed approval. And so, he had little reason to be too worried about the outcome.

Surprisingly, Cape – who also published his brother's travel books – were not too keen. The general opinion of their manuscript readers had been to turn it down. But pressure from Peter and the fact that Fleming had made the eponymous Jonathan Cape a personal friend got him past first base. Cape would publish it after all.

The book first appeared in the shops on 13 April 1953 and was immediately placed on the bestseller lists, proving that the publisher's readers knew absolutely nothing about public taste. The rest is history – reprint after reprint and thousands in the bank!

***

James Bond – 007 as Fleming dubbed him – was never really a spy who is sent out to gather and then report back the information he has pulled together. His 00 prefix gives him the liberty to kill as he sees fit, thus making him, in Fleming's words, 'a blunt instrument' to be thrown at a problem. Whatever his nomenclature, Fleming created a compelling character who would grow, in time, to be a monster who hunted and haunted him. But not yet.

To the end of his life, Bond remained a romanticised version of Ian Fleming himself. He had spent most of the war years behind a desk, more M than Bond, sending out agents to kill, maim and assassinate, the very tasks that Fleming would have liked to carry out himself. Now, through his literary creation he could realise his dreams, not just in the violence and danger Bond would have to face but in the vitally important area of good living and womanising!

The name James Bond was taken from an American ornithologist who had written Fleming's favourite book about West Indian birds. It was, as Fleming described it, 'the dullest name I ever heard'.[5] In contrast to his dull name, however, Bond was a masterful creation, all action and energy, propelled by instincts that would have been alien to most people.

The character was actually something of a composite, consisting of large elements of Fleming's brother Peter and the famous Sidney Reilly, 'Ace of Spies', who had disappeared in Soviet Russia in the early 1920s. Fleming himself made up a significant part of the character, at least Fleming as he imagined himself. So, too, did the former British Second World War double agent Alan Dusko Popov.

There were many others. For looks, Fleming pictured him to be something like the Hollywood singer and film star Hoagy Carmichael.

Composite characters were important for Fleming. Le Chiffre was based partly on Aleister Crowley, the great necromancer and evil influence of the age. Bond's chief, known only by the letter M, was partly drawn from Fleming's own chief during the war, Admiral Godfrey, and partly from Sir Stewart Menzies, head of MI6 – a man who was known throughout the service as M. It has been suggested that there were also elements of Eve Fleming in the more demanding or dictatorial aspects of M's character.

Spy, secret agent, hit man, whatever he was, Fleming's Bond took the world of spy literature by storm. The genre had been languishing in the doldrums since the end of the war, never having moved on from the days of John Buchan and, more regretfully, since Sapper and his infamous Bulldog Drummond.

The 1920s and '30s had seen a huge upsurge in spy literature but, unfortunately, so much of it was of poor quality. *Casino Royale* gave the genre the kick in the pants that it deserved, returning it to the hedonistic days of Buchan's Richard Hannay and Somerset Maugham's Ashenden.

Reviews of Fleming's work were excellent and continued to be positive for the first five Bond books. All sections of society, from the great and famous to the unknown, waited eagerly for the next novel to appear. It seemed as if Fleming could do no wrong.

Senator, later US President, John F Kennedy declared that Fleming was his favourite writer, naming *From Russia with Love* as the Bond book he loved best. The renowned novelist and thriller writer Raymond Chandler was also a great fan, writing that Fleming was 'the most forceful and driving writer of thrillers in England'.[6]

Casino Royale was followed by *Live and Let Die, Moonraker, Diamonds are Forever* and *From Russia with Love*. All of them were peopled by interesting, even fascinating, characters and, with the exception of *Moonraker*, were all set in exotic locations. Bond's opponents began with SMERSH but soon evolved into SPECTRE, a criminal organisation with fingers into all sorts of crimes. From stealing coding machines to holding the world to ransom, Fleming's creation of the international gangster empire was a masterstroke.

Bond's enemies hardly mattered to the reading public. As long as the chief villain was almost – the key word is 'almost' – a match for Bond, they were happy. They could not get enough of the world Fleming had created, a combination of romance, luxury and danger where the hero – and the villains, too, come to that – would lead lives that were immensely attractive and hugely desirable.

At this distance, it is hard to know which came first, the hedonism of the sixties or the series of Bond novels that reflected and caught it. Read now, the lists of exotic food and drink enjoyed by Bond, the range of countries he visited, the trials and tribulations of US Customs, station stops on his journey south to St Petersburg in *Live and Let Die* are, like so much else in virtually all of the books, totters on the edge of boredom. At the time of publication, however, such details were exactly what a luxury-deprived reading public wanted.

Fleming was intrigued, maybe even obsessed, by America. He visited the country many times, revelling in the brittle wealth and garishness of the towns and cities he encountered. From his much-loved New York to the retirement paradise of St Petersburg, America in all its glory is presented to the reader. It was a heady mix and, again, the reading public snapped it up.

It is quite amazing how many times the USA appears, either as the main location for a Bond novel or as something of a 'supporting cast.' In this Fleming reflects much of the interest and attitude of the British people. America, about which most of them had known little until the GIs arrived in the 1940s, was increasingly seen as an ideal, an exotic ideal to which they could yearn and admire.

Fleming doesn't just visit the country, he ensures that the British secret service, in the shape of his hero, has credibility and a strength that was very far from reality. In fact, Bond does not just help America, he saves it:

> He stopped Dr No from "toppling" a crucial American missile test (1962), prevented Goldfinger from making the Fort Knox gold reserves radioactive (1964); thwarted Largo's attempt to blow up Miami (*Thunderball*, 1965) and Blofeld's to destroy Washington (the villain rejects Kansa – "the world might not notice." (*Diamonds are Forever*, 1971)[7]

Above all, Fleming made sure that the world in which his creations lived and died was both fantasy and yet real. His paperback publisher Pan even cashed in by producing *The Book of Bond: Every Man His Own 007*, a continuation of the fantasy where everyone could adapt his lifestyle to be just like the dashing secret agent. From the clothing to wear to the car you had to drive, the Bond persona was intricately laid out for would-be aficionados to take, adopt and use.

Fleming had imposed an arduous task on himself. Only when he was well into the process did he realise that what he had set for himself was a target that was well-nigh impossible. He would write a Bond book every year, using the two-month break in Jamaica to carry out the job. Inevitably, what he had created was a production line and with time, as might be expected, the quality of what he was able to produce began to wane.

The production line was not one which produced cars like Henry Ford's factories where every vehicle was exactly the same as the ones before and after. Here there was a human element involved. And the human spirit was always a transitory element. There is no denying that, from a literary perspective, the standard of the first five books was excellent but thereafter the quality dropped off considerably.

The books continued to be bestsellers and brought Fleming large quantities of money and fame. Both were always important to him.

Despite the clear drop-off in standard, many of them became the works that people, fans and general readers alike, immediately recognised and associated with Fleming. Most readers were not bothered about the drop in literary quality and simply accepted each book as another adventure in the James Bond saga. *Dr No, Goldfinger, For Your Eyes Only, Thunderball, The Spy Who Loved Me, On Her Majesty's Secret Service* and *You Only Live Twice* all helped to create and extend the literary life of James Bond.

To a large extent, quality in this second tranche of books was replaced by shock and by sensationalism. The writing remained sharp but now Fleming took his formulaic approach and twisted it to what the readers seemed to expect – violence and brutality worthy of Bulldog Drummond himself:

> More and more they were touched by sadism, and the deaths of some of his characters were bizarre to say the least – Doctor No is despatched by being smothered in bird droppings.[8]

As early as *Live and Let Die,* the second Bond novel, torture scenes which are central to almost every Bond story, become horrific. When Mr Big's compatriot Tee-Hee Johnson tortures Bond by bending back his finger until it breaks, you can almost sense the delight of Fleming in the pain to which Bond has to submit. Bond limits himself to a groan but faints and the reader feels like doing so as well.

By the time his fifth Bond novel, *From Russia with Love*, reached the book shops Fleming was tired and totally fed up with his creation. The production line approach made this inevitable, the writer churning out thriller after thriller regardless of his own wishes, intent only on meeting his own self-imposed deadline. Fleming now wanted to write other things even though the reading public was clamouring for more Bond. There was only one thing to do.

Just as Arthur Conan Doyle had killed off Sherlock Holmes by having him plunge to his death over the Reichenbach Falls, so Fleming decided that he would do something similar with Bond. He forgot, deliberately or by accident, that public pressure had forced Conan Doyle to bring Holmes back to life.

As it turned out Fleming did not go that far. When all the chips were finally down, he did not quite have the courage to kill off James Bond. He was too valuable a cash cow and without him, poverty again seemed to beckon. And yet – and yet!

The end of *From Russia with Love* is suitably ambiguous, the reader being left very much up in the air. Bond has despatched Red Grant on the Orient Express but now, in a luxury hotel in Venice, there is a question to be asked. Is Bond killed or has he somehow managed to survive the poisoned blade of arch-villain Rosa Klebb?

> Now he had to gasp for breath. Again, his hand moved up towards his cold face … Bond felt his knees begin to buckle.
> He said, or thought he said, "I've already got the loveliest …"
> Bond pivoted slowly on his heel and crashed headlong to the wine-red floor.[9]

In the end, Fleming gave Bond a reprieve and brought him back for further adventures. Again, he forgot the experience of Conan Doyle. As one Edwardian wit had earlier declared 'Holmes may have survived going over the Falls but he was never the same man afterwards'. Bond returned in *Dr No*, followed by a further eight books but, quality reduced, he really was never quite the same again.

Sadly, with the publication of *Dr No*, the reviewers and critics turned against Fleming like a pack of murderous wolves. Admittedly, the literary quality of the works had taken a turn for the worse but the virulence of the reviewers is hard to explain – certainly after the glowing reception of the first five volumes.

One vicious review under the headline 'Sex, Snobbery and Sadism' gives an indication of what can only be described as the violent reception of the book. The reviewer condemns the basic structure and content of the story, taking Fleming to task in a prose essay which gives more than a little hint of personal affront and dislike:

> (The book has) the sadism of a schoolboy bully, the mechanical, two-dimensional sex-longings of a frustrated adolescent, and the crude snob-cravings of a suburban adult ... Mr Fleming has no literary skill, the construction of the book is chaotic, and entire individuals and situations are inserted and then forgotten, in a haphazard manner.[10]

As might be expected in a personality so fragile as Fleming's the reviews and the abuse hurt. He went into a personal and creative decline that, ultimately, proved fatal. Fleming had written and delivered *Goldfinger* before *Dr No* was published and duly savaged by the critics. Luckily, he found some solace in the rather gentler reviews that *Goldfinger* brought.

However, the first book written after *Dr No* was a collection of short stories, *For Your Eyes Only*. It was, as he had feared, mauled by the critics, perhaps deservedly. He had lost heart and, more importantly, lost interest in his creation.

Fleming toyed with despatching Bond for good in several future books, notably *You Only Live Twice* and *The Man with the Golden Gun*. He never quite managed it and, in the end, a heart attack finished off Bond's creator before he could deal with 007.

Ian Fleming died at the Kent and Canterbury Hospital in the early morning of 12 April 1964 after suffering a fatal coronary at the hotel where he was staying in Canterbury. He was just 53 years old. His last two Bond stories, *The Man with the Golden Gun* and the two short novellas *Octopussy and Living Daylights* were published posthumously, as was the book written for his son Caspar as a bedtime treat from Ian – *Chitty-Chitty-Bang-Bang*.

Neither of the final two Bond volumes was really ready for publication and there is little doubt that Fleming would have edited them severely, maybe even have rewritten them, given time. He did not have the opportunity.

***

The creation of James Bond made Fleming a rich man. At the time of his death, his estate was estimated to be worth well over four million pounds (by modern monetary standards). The money was important, Fleming had never denied that, but significantly, he had made a remarkable addition to the world of spy literature. He had undoubtedly resurrected the genre, brought it up to date after a rather dismal decade and made it more popular than it had ever been.

There is no doubt that the Bond books were sexist, misogynist, racist and increasingly obsessed with violence. But they were hugely popular and the lifestyle of the main character reflected the standard of living that most people of the time wanted to achieve. The sixties and Bond? They go together like fish and chips – or, as Fleming would have preferred it, caviar and vodka.

It had not been done without effort and a degree of pain. For example, his novel *Thunderball* was at the centre of a controversy which almost threatened to de-rail Fleming completely. He was never one to deal easily with problems and this new book was full of them.

Originally emerging from a discussion on a sun-drenched beach in Jamaica, the book was a novelisation of a screenplay designed and discussed by Fleming and several others including screenwriters and producers Jack Whittingham, Kevin McClory, Ernest Cuneo and Fleming's long-time friend and confidant Ivar Bryce.

In March 1961 Whittington read an advance copy of *Thunderball* and was appalled to find that he and the others involved in the original discussion had not been recognised or mentioned anywhere in the acknowledgements. Whittington and McClory immediately came up with an injunction to stop publication. The matter was eventually settled out of court with Fleming claiming rights on the book, Whittington and McClory being named as co-writers of the film script.

Perhaps the greatest sadness of Fleming's life is the fact that he died just as one of the most lucrative and successful film franchises of all time was beginning to make its mark.

In July 1961 he had sold the film rights for six feature films to Harry Saltzman with an option to purchase the titles, if not the exact wording of each future book, as they were written. Beginning with *Dr No*, the success of the Bond films was phenomenal, as all the world knows!

In fact, *Dr No* was not the first appearance of Bond on the screen. A Canadian television adaptation of *Casino Royale* in 1955, with Peter Lorre playing the part of Le Chiffre – to whom must go the credit for the first screen Bond villain – and little-known actor Barry Nelson appearing as 'Jimmy' Bond, transposed into an American, got there first.

This first 'silver screen' appearance was just an hour-long drama but it added to money-making events like radio broadcasts and comic strips in daily newspapers that kept Fleming and Bond in the public eye throughout the 1950s and 1960s. Spin-offs included James Bond Jnr and there was even a female version, Jane Bond, a forerunner of the more renowned Modesty Blaze, who appeared for a while in one of Britain's daily papers!

By the time Fleming's final books began to hit the stands James Bond had made his mark and was beginning to fade in terms of public acceptance and popularity. He was, some might say, past his sell-by date, at least in the moral sense.

For the final years of his life, Fleming's books continued to sell well, particularly after President Kennedy announced his approval and as the steady stream of Bond films began to hit the cinema screens. The films are still being made and released.

The films made international stars out of Sean Connery and Roger Moore, both of whom played Bond in their own idiosyncratic ways, although, increasingly during the tenure of Roger Moore, the film scripts bore little resemblance to the original stories.

By the late 1960s, the world had turned away from so many of the standards that Fleming had taken for granted, although not, it must be admitted, from the gadget-ridden glossy films. It was not just the out-of-date views of Fleming – and Bond – about women, there were many other problems:

> Socialism is synonymous with crime, unions are fifth columnists of the Soviet Union ... and negroes are superstitious, murderous lackeys.[11]

A sweeping judgement, perhaps, but then Fleming's views of left-wing politics, women and the race issue were equally as sweeping and generalised.

Fleming, like his hero, was of his time but even now, nearly sixty years after his death, his popularity as a writer of spy fiction remains large. His books have never been allowed to go out of print, his easy and fluent writing style finding legions of new fans every generation.

This continued popularity of the author and his creations is partly due to the regular release of one Bond film after the other, filled with stunts and gadgets galore. Purists might deplore this slant on their hero but there is no doubt that the films, however way-out they might be, have helped maintain Ian Fleming's position at the top of the espionage writing pantheon.

Even at the height of his popularity, the role of Fleming's fictional British Secret Service – and Bond in particular – had evolved into something that was out of proportion to the standing of the country. That was part of the appeal in the post-war years when everything that Britain had fought for – Empire, status, worldwide acclaim – seemed to have diminished, if not totally disappeared.

In a world gone out of shape, at least as far as Fleming was concerned, the creation of James Bond gave the British people comfort and something to cling to on the dark, cold nights of international mediocrity:

> Like George and the Dragon, Bond has indeed become a myth. And myths don't die, easily, especially when they flatter us with the idea that Britannia can still punch above her weight ... suspending disbelief is, of course, the name of the game.[12]

Quite apart from the films, the books are still read and no survey of spy literature would be complete without the inclusion of Ian Fleming. He deserves his place in The Triumvirate where, in the words of critic and reviewer William Cook he and his creation remain the 'Bulldog Drummond of the jet age'.[13]

Chapter Eight

A Modest Little Secret Agent

In the wake of Ian Fleming's *Casino Royale* and its successors, a whole host of spy novels hit the bookshops. Many were imitations of Bond and his world, pale or otherwise; several of the more interesting ones took a diametrically opposed stance to the elegance and social superiority of Fleming's hero and many critics regard this trend as the birth of the anti-hero in the field of espionage novels.

Whatever their thrust, the plethora of new spy novels showed that within the space of just one book James Bond had become the standard, against which every writer of espionage tales would be judged. And one fact quickly became clear. Where they were good, the books were of an exceptional quality; where they were bad, they were dire.

If the pre-Bond world of spy fiction had been little more than a regurgitation of William Le Queux, E Phillips Oppenheim, Sapper et al then the post-war – and post-Bond – glut of espionage stories was a good deal more acceptable to the critics. Many of the books took 007, complete with all his affectations and sexist quirks, and turned him inside out in order to create a marketable hero!

Ian Fleming had given his readers what they wanted – very little spy work but considerable effort on food, drink and exotic locations. That was perfectly understandable in the wake of war and the deprivation and hardship that most people in Britain had endured.

Quite apart from the hedonism of the Bond books, one significant reason for 007's phenomenal success was undoubtedly the poor quality of 'spy offerings' in the 1930s. That poor standard continued into the 1940s and even into the early 1950s and '60s – with the exception of Eric Ambler, Somerset Maugham and one or two others.

True, between 1939 and 1945 there had been a little matter of a war to be won, there is no way to hide that fact. But, even so, the stream of second-rate offerings was monumentally bad:

> The most prolific period of the spy story was between 1914 and 1939 but it was very far from being a golden age of espionage fiction. Hundreds of authors produced thousands of stories, short and long, during that quarter of a century ... Some of the stories were competent, one or two like Maugham's *Ashenden* were first class, the vast majority was mediocre and many were appallingly bad.[1]

The fifties, sixties and seventies were marked by what was euphemistically known as the Cold War. In fact, the period was anything but 'cold', the tensions and pressures of the time proving to be a more than fertile stamping ground for the writers of spy fiction.

Real-life spies and double agents gave the espionage writers much to ponder. The activities of Kim Philby and his fellow members of the Cambridge Five, the tragic pairing of the seemingly innocuous Ethel and Julius Rosenberg, double or even triple agent Oleg Penkovsky, atom spy Klaus Fuchs and so many more rivalled whatever the fiction writers could produce. It was hard going but they certainly gave it everything they had got.

In the post-war period, Eric Ambler and Graham Greene both produced fine examples of spy fiction, notably Greene's *The Quiet American* and, breaking new ground, the satirical and blatantly funny *Our Man in Havana*. The leading exponents of the art, however, and following in the wake of Ian Fleming were probably Len Deighton and Frederick Forsyth.

Deighton and Forsyth were markedly different writers from Fleming, different in style and in values, but they both attracted something of a cult following that was reminiscent of Fleming at the height of his popularity.

Deighton pitched his hero – nameless in his books, dubbed Harry Palmer in the films which quickly followed the successful novels – at the opposite end of the market from Bond. Palmer was no public school educated officer; he was a non-commissioned officer from the British Army. He had spent a period in prison and was blessed with decidedly working-class values and attitudes along with a healthy distrust of his upper-crust controllers.

The only similarity between Deighton and Fleming lies in the banality of their heroes' names, Harry Palmer and James Bond. That banality was deliberate on the part of Fleming but was certainly not a Deighton invention as he had originally given his central character no name at all. As far as he was concerned the ordinariness of his hero was implicit in everything he said and did.

Michael Caine caught the character perfectly in films such as *The Ipcress File* and *Funeral in Berlin.* As a counter to James Bond, Palmer is beautifully crafted and created. Even so, Deighton's real love lay not in his characters but in the technology of spying and its application to the espionage task in the late twentieth century. Once again, the detail offered to the reader does not detract but, rather, adds to the interest and believability of the plots.

Frederick Forsyth took a totally different approach. In his classic 1960s epistle *The Odessa File* his hero is not a spy or secret agent, he is a working journalist with an axe to grind and a task to carry out. He manages to do this quite successfully, saving Israel from the terror weapons of Egypt and exposing several members of the Nazi-based Odessa organisation.

Forsyth's *The Day of the Jackal* takes yet another, remarkably different view of the spy novel. It installs the central character, not as the James Bond-style hero but as the villain of the piece, a professional contract killer who stalks General De Gaulle on behalf of the OAS. He is amoral but totally committed to his task, in this case assassinating De Gaulle.

The failure of the Jackal's plan is inevitable – De Gaulle, as we know, was not assassinated – but it renders the conclusion out of character for the assassin and therefore makes the finale somewhat unbelievable.

De Gaulle bends forward at the crucial moment as he awards a medal, the Jackal misses his shot and the otherwise perfect killer fails or falls at the last fence. Given his meticulous preparations and planning this failure is hardly believable. Nevertheless, the crux of the story comes not in the final scene but in the build-up to that moment and the infinite care the villain takes over the plan – which makes that ending so much more unbelievable.

Other notable writers of spy fiction in the late twentieth century include Robert Harris whose book *Enigma* was concerned with one of the truly great discoveries of the Second World War. Tom Clancy's debut novel *The Hunt for Red October* became a phenomenal success, undoubtedly aided by a magnificent Sean Connery film of the same name. Perhaps the most important recent writer in the genre was Stieg Larsson, author of books like *The Girl with the Dragon Tattoo*, but there are many who deny his right to be called a spy writer.

The most significant character to emerge on the espionage novel scene in the final days of the Cold War, however, was a small and seemingly insignificant individual by the name of George Smiley. The creation of John le Carré, real name David Cornwell, Smiley remains perhaps the perfect spy and a fitting memorial to le Carré, the final member of The Triumvirate.

***

David John Moore Cornwell was born in the seaside town of Poole in Dorset, on 19 October 1931. His immediate family relationships and, as a consequence, his early life was traumatic and nothing if not 'adventurous'.

His father was christened Ronald Thomas Archibald Cornwell but was almost universally referred to as Ronnie. As everyone who ever came into contact with Ronnie knew only too well, he was a crook and a con man, a charming rogue who had connections with the infamous Kray twins from London's East End.

Ronnie Cornwell might not have had the murderous streak of the Krays but he was every bit as determined to make his money out of other people's mistakes and greed. Indeed, he virtually dedicated his life to it. He was full of bonhomie and incredibly personable, even those he had conned finding it impossible to dislike him.

Declared bankrupt in 1954 and, eventually, jailed for insurance fraud, Ronnie was constantly in debt. The need for money ran like a river in spate through his life, constantly affecting his family and friends, his children in particular.

Ronnie was far from the perfect role model for his young son but some good did eventually come out of the relationship when David, then writing as John le Carré, created and re-modelled him in *A Perfect Spy* as the dubious but enchanting Rick Pym. The book is probably le Carré's best 'non-Smiley' piece of work, centred on the espionage world but going one step beyond it to examine the motivation of the main character and detailing the way spies are formed or created.

It is always dangerous to associate a fiction writer's productions with fact. However, it remains abundantly clear that Ronnie was the model for Rick Pym in *The Perfect Spy*. He is the significant – although fatally – flawed father figure to Magnus Pym, the hero in this emotionally taut piece of writing. It was probably le Carré's most personal, most autobiographical book, a novel which is almost doubling as a piece of memoir writing. It presents a harrowing picture, one which shows the pain to which the young David Cornwell was exposed during his childhood.

Cornwell's mother, Olive Moore Cornwell, effectively passed out of her son's life when he was just five years old. Marriage to the charming Ronnie, who abused – both physically and emotionally – whenever and however he pleased was far from easy. In fact, it was impossible.

Knowing that he had been unfaithful from the earliest days of their marriage, and was never likely to change his ways in the future, in 1936 Olive simply walked out on her husband, on the family home and on her children. She literally went out of the door and locked it carefully behind her. She took up with another man, made a life for herself in East Anglia and never returned to Dorset.

Her new relationship with John Hill seemed to be more successful but, even so, it was perhaps inevitable that Olive should retain a degree of affection for Ronnie. That was part of the appeal and character of the man. She would arrange to meet him surreptitiously in London hotels, listening to and laughing at his tall tales and even, on occasions, sleeping with him.

Such might have been the way with a charming confidence trickster like Ronnie but it was another sixteen years before contact between Olive and her son David Cornwell was re-established and by then they had each become set in their ways and the damage was done. In whatever way they re-established their togetherness it was never going to be the close, fulfilling and mutually beneficial relationship that each of them probably needed.

During his childhood David might have been deprived of a mother's love but security and comfort were still there, provided for him by Tony, his elder brother. It was a substitute form of protection and it was something that the young David Cornwell never forgot.

With Tony protecting David, the irresponsible Ronnie sailed blithely on. He certainly had delusions of grandeur and at one stage even fought a parliamentary election at Yarmouth on behalf of the Liberal Party. He lost! Although he promised, like General MacArthur was later to do in the Philippines that 'he would be back', it had been a temporary aberration and politics disappeared into the far reaches of Ronnie's brain.

As a result of Ronnie's vision of the world, David and his siblings – elder brother Tony, younger half-brother Rupert and half-sister Charlotte – were sent to the finest public schools of the day. As might be expected with someone as ambivalent as Ronnie, paying for the education of his children remained a problem even though he had agreed to their placements in the first place. He viewed such interruptions to his basic routine as a necessary evil and, as might be expected, attempted to avoid coughing up the school fees whenever they were demanded.

It was a fractured, disabled childhood but David and his siblings came through it. Indeed, their battle to survive led to success on a significant scale, confirming the old cliché that battling against adversity merely confirms the quality of a person's character.

Apart from David and his achievements as a writer, the other children in Ronnie and Olive's two homes and two separate lives all did well.

Tony Cornwell became an advertising executive, played county cricket for Dorset and later made a life for himself in the USA. Charlotte became an actress, starring in many stage performances and in the hit TV series *Rock Follies* alongside Rula Lenska and Julie Covington. Rupert rose to become the Washington Bureau Chief for *The Independent* newspaper. Success indeed – Ronnie was undoubtedly proud but it did not stop him touching them all up for loans!

Coming from such a dysfunctional family with a father who was always just one step ahead of the law it was inevitable that David and his brother Tony, always his closest sibling, should develop survival strategies. Ronnie's perpetual 'wheeling and dealing', painful as it may have been at the time, did have positive moments for the future spy and espionage writer. Cornwell/le Carré was well aware of the debt:

> "I'm a liar," he explains. "Born to lying, bred to it, trained to it by an industry that lies for a living, practised in it as a novelist."[2]

Being somewhat careful with the truth was one way to survive but the hurt of abandonment still went deep. As with all seismic pains, it remained with him through childhood and adolescence. Arguably that hurt, that feeling of being let down, never left him even when he developed into one of the truly great writers of the twentieth century.

In 1952 he met his mother for the first time in nearly twenty years, her address having been given to him by his uncle, the Liberal MP Alec Glassey. Mother and son met on the platform of Ipswich railway station, a suitably transient location for the reunion. The meeting was a little strained, as might be expected, but it was contact and connection of a sort. Even so, his feelings of hurt and abandonment continued.

Strong feelings of betrayal haunted David Cornwell's childhood, adolescence and adulthood, lasting until his final days. Then, in old age, he became so violently opposed to the Brexit process, viewing Britain's withdrawal as the ultimate mistake and stab in the back, that he fell back on his family's Irish antecedence and changed his nationality to Irish. He had little time for the British politicians who had engineered the exit from Europe. Boris Johnson, then in his pre-Prime Minister days and the man who engineered the withdrawal was, in his opinion, 'a pig ignorant foreign secretary'.[3]

The two themes that were to appear constantly and consistently as major issues in almost all of le Carré's fiction, almost overriding and subsuming the espionage element of the books, were abandonment and betrayal – hardly surprising when you consider the traumas of his youth and adolescence. They, perhaps more than anything else, were what made his writing so special, lifting it out of the ordinary, run-of-the-mill spy stories of the fifties and sixties.

***

David Cornwell began his formal education at St Andrews Preparatory School near Pangbourne, a traditional enough start for children of the privileged classes who were destined for the Public School system. The prep school provided education of a sort but, more significantly, prepared its pupils for the life they would 'enjoy' in the waiting Public Schools of their choice.

In 1945, the final year of the war, David Cornwell moved on, as custom demanded, to his chosen Public School at Sherbourne. It was better, more amenable, than the prep school but despite the efforts of his elder brother to protect and guard him, David was still unhappy at Sherbourne. He particularly disliked his Housemaster, R S Thompson, and was appalled by the atmosphere of 'muscular Christianity' that pervaded the school.

Boarding school was one more unpleasant aspect of childhood and adolescence, something to be endured rather than enjoyed. Cornwell, however, was not the sort of character to accept such challenges lightly. He saw little purpose in the discipline of Thompson and the all-school ethos of physicality which had been created by the senior staff.

It was not that he was an out-and-out rebel. Indeed, he later recounted that he had done quite well at the school but retained a realistic view of his time there:

> I wasn't a failure at school, far from it; captain of things, winner of school prizes, potential golden boy ... very probably I blamed the school for my woes.[4]

Unhappy and unfulfilled, he stuck at it while all the time counting the days and months until he could finally leave. This he finally managed to do in 1948 when he enrolled at the University of Bern in Switzerland in order to study languages.

His stay in Switzerland was short-lived but he did find time to enjoy a new pastime and interest. Like Buchan and Fleming before him, he fell in love with the mountains of Europe, high-haloed places where he could reach out and touch eternity.

And like Fleming, he became particularly adept at skiing, so adept that he was on the fringe of selection for the British Downhill Racing team. He later spent a brief period as temporary ski instructor at Chamonix – no mean achievement for any Briton at that time.

He also found time to fall in love. This was with Alison Ann Sharp and, as with everything he did, it soon became an all-consuming interest. The love affair was a full-on, serious relationship, one which eventually resulted in their formal engagement and marriage.

After just one year in Europe Cornwell was recalled to Britain for his obligatory stint of National Service. The army realised his gift for languages and, after being plucked from Basic Training and awarded a commission, David Cornwell found himself posted to what was still Allied-occupied Austria. He left for Austria in March 1951, taking up a post in the town of Graz. He was now working for the Army Intelligence Corps.

As a field security officer, one of his jobs was to interrogate defectors and refugees who had fled across the border, braving the Iron Curtain and the East German guards to find a better life in the west. Most of them were genuine enough, but in the eyes of the government and military, there was always the danger of the USSR slipping agents in amongst what was soon a seething mass of fleeing humanity.

Cornwell also 'ran' a string of informants, men and women who passed on information, most of it fairly low grade and of little real value, to the Allies. All of this activity, however, was his first contact with the 'secret' world of spies and agents. And the clandestine world, even on the fringes, perfectly suited his personality.

At the end of his two-year stint in the Army, Cornwell returned to England, taking up a place at Lincoln College, Oxford. He was a bright and talented young man and at Oxford, his subject was once again foreign languages, French and German in particular.

Like many men and women who had been touched by the lure of espionage, he was unable to totally push away the secret world and, despite having supposedly finished his stint in the army, at Oxford he continued his connections with espionage. On the surface, he was a typical student of the time but what no one realised was that he was also still actively involved in spying for MI6. Once again Cornwell's efforts were of a fairly minor nature.

He was charged with reporting on the university left-wing groups and identifying any potential Soviet agents or collaborators amongst the students. It was hardly arduous work and the students did not suspect that their activities were being monitored by one of their number.

Taking a break from academe, David Cornwell spent a brief period teaching at Millfield School in Somerset, an establishment more renowned for its sporting prowess than any academic success, before returning to Oxford. There, in 1956, he duly graduated with a 'first' in foreign languages.

Then came a two-year interlude teaching French and German at Eton College before giving up the pretence of 'posing as an educationalist' and becoming a formal employee of MI5. It was, perhaps, an inevitable move. He was twenty-six years old and the world of espionage, as he later commented, seemed to be something to which he had been born.

For the next few years, David Cornwell was happily involved with the running of agents, interrogation work and traditional spy activities like phone tapping and break-ins. Married, now, to Ann Sharp, he was living in a house that he and his wife had struggled to buy in Great Missenden, commuting into London every day.

At this time, it was Ann, not David, who was the one with literary pretensions. She was determined to become a published writer but despite support from her husband she received little more than polite, although encouraging, rejection letters from the editors of the magazines and the BBC programmes to which she sent her stories and plays.

In time Ann's lack of success, compared to her husband's monumental achievements, would begin to grate and, eventually, lead to jealousy. Not for the moment, however.

In 1960 David Cornwell transferred to MI6, a move which inevitably meant a foreign posting, and in due course, with the cover of Second Secretary, he was sent to the British Embassy in Bonn. Initially, he went alone but within a few months, once accommodation had been sorted out, he was joined by his wife Ann and their two children.

The quiet, sedate West German town was then the capital of free Germany, famous only for being the home of Ludwig Beethoven. Perhaps unexpectedly, it was to feature as the central location in David's later book *A Small Town in Germany*.

Despite its sleepy, unremarkable appearance, to begin with, he and Ann were happy in 'Bloody Bonn' as the British agents and Embassy staff affectionately called the place. After the struggle of trying to pay a mortgage in England, this was a charming, almost rural interlude in the life of the young couple. 'Expat' living suited them both.

A third child was born to the couple and, more importantly, the beginnings of literary invention were stirring in Cornwell's brain. He had not previously shown any inclination to become a full-time writer, leaving that ambition with his wife.

However, the business of espionage and running agents seemed to appeal to his imagination and when he made the move to Bonn for some reason the sleepy West German town set free his creative instincts. He had not been long in Germany before he made a momentous decision. He could – and he would – become a writer.

Whatever the value of Bonn, the posting was a positive one. He did not know it at the time but the world of David Cornwell – and the world of spy fiction – was about to change forever.

Chapter Nine

Smiley Takes the Prize

In fact, David Cornwell had begun writing his first novel whilst still employed by MI5. It was entitled *Call for the Dead*, a mystery story or thriller rather than a tale of espionage, but a tale which did at least feature the modest and self-deprecating George Smiley as a retired spy investigating the apparent suicide of a dead communist. The book may have been written before he left MI5 but it was not published until 1961, by which time Cornwell had moved on to employment with Britain's overseas secret department.

Regulations at the time prevented MI5 and MI6 employees writing and publishing books under their own names. Cornwell was also obliged to present his book for approval by his senior officers. That nod of agreement was soon given and the man who was to become probably the greatest spy novelist of the twentieth century saw his first work in print appear under the somewhat exotic pseudonym of John le Carré.

In keeping with his love for foreign languages, it was perhaps inevitable that either French or German would provide the pseudonym he was looking for. Le Carré is French for 'the square', a term which fitted Cornwell and his characters on so many different levels and interpretations. Senior Foreign Office staff might have quickly given their approval to the book but Victor Gollancz, the publishers, were not so happy with the pseudonym by which he had decided to be known:

> The publishers were not enthusiastic with the pseudonym David had chosen, and proposed that instead he should adopt one made up from Anglo-Saxon monosyllables

suggesting an American provenance, such as Chuck Smith or Hank Brown; but David resisted this advice.[1]

Cornwell was undoubtedly right in his decision. It remains impossible to see *Smiley's People, Tinker Tailor Soldier Spy* or any of the later books appearing above a name like Chuck Smith. Le Carré it was and le Carré it would stay.

Call for the Dead was soon followed by a second detective story, *A Murder of Quality*. It again featured George Smiley but unlike the first book which had hovered around the fringes of the espionage world, this was a pure detective story.

Both books were successful, garnering a range of positive reviews, but nothing quite prepared le Carré/Cornwell for what was about to happen next. His third book, *The Spy Who Came in from the Cold*, exceeded both his and his publishers' expectations and was an immediate smash hit. The book had been well puffed, given huge pre-publication publicity with the result that the reading public was waiting expectantly for its appearance.

Pre-ordering meant that *The Spy Who Came in from the Cold* had to be reprinted three times before it even appeared in the book shops. And when Victor Gollancz, the original publisher, sold the paperback rights to Pan it was clear that le Carré and Gollancz had a best seller on their hands. By the end of November 1963 over 50,000 advance copies of the book had been ordered and when the book finally appeared in the book shops sales spiralled into the stratosphere.

The character of George Smiley, who had been the central figure of the first two books, had been based on a number of different people known to le Carré, notably Sir Maurice Oldfield and John Bingham. Alec Leamas, the central character of *The Spy Who Came in from the Cold*, had a very different pedigree altogether.

Le Carré was apparently sitting in a bar at Heathrow Airport when a middle-aged man, bedraggled and clad in a dirty, stained raincoat appeared in the doorway. His eyes, the ever-watchful writer noticed, were dead. He padded across to the bar, fished around in his pocket for money to pay for his drink – and in that instant, Alec Leamas was born.[2]

If George Smiley had been created as an alternative to James Bond, Alec Leamas laid utter waste to Ian Fleming's creation. Leamas is a man at the end of his tether, someone who is set up and deliberately 'left out in the cold' by the very people who are supposed to protect him – the British Secret Service, the Circus as it is known in le Carré's espionage world. The book lays bare the intricacies of the espionage business, clearly showing that there are no good or bad guys in that universe and that one side is just as devious as the other.

The book was written at a point of crisis in le Carré's life. He had grown unhappy with his career in MI6 – as the briefest reading of the book, filled as it is with disappointment and regret, will show. He would have happily resigned his post but that was something he could not afford to do. He needed money in order to survive and with a growing family, it was clear that requirement would not go away any time soon. As a result, the feeling of being shackled to the job became a niggle which quickly grew and soon developed into an open sore.

That was not his only concern. He was also unfulfilled at home where Ann had become increasingly envious of his literary success. Such was her resentment that she refused to type any of his manuscripts after having assisted in the first two. The result of that withdrawal of assistance meant that he was forced to use his secretaries at work in order to produce an acceptable MS. With the publication of the first two books Ann's involvement in the literary world of John le Carré abruptly and succinctly ended, the microcosm of his writer's existence perfectly reflecting the problems in Cornwell's macro world.

It was not just professional jealousy that was coming between them. Ann and David were growing more and more bored with each other. He had already found himself engaged in an affair with another member of the Embassy staff and his personal situation reflected much of the angst in the world at that time.

Disgruntlement and unhappiness pervade almost every page of *The Spy Who Came in from the Cold*, where the emotional and physical effect of the Berlin Wall, erected in 1962 as le Carré was just beginning to write the book, were symbolic of a man and a situation out of balance with the world. He visited Berlin and was appalled by the effect of the Wall which cut people off from their families and symbolised the cultural and political differences between western and eastern Europe.

This was the time of the Cuban Missile Crisis and the Bay of Pigs fiasco, an era when the sense of imminent destruction was prevalent in all government circles. It hovers over every word of le Carré's new book. Dark days indeed!

Above all, this was also a time of betrayal. A number of British officials and agents had recently been exposed as Soviet spies, amongst them John Vassall and, perhaps most damaging of all, Kim Philby. An accepted and experienced senior espionage operator, Philby was the so-called Third Man in the trio of double agents – later to become five – headed by Guy Burgess and Donald Maclean.

The Philby affair shocked the complacent world of British empiricism and put a barrier between Britain and the USA which was to last for many years. Cornwell felt the betrayal quite deeply, almost at a personal level. That feeling of being betrayed and let down was to surface in *The Spy Who Came in from the Cold* and, in particular, *Tinker Tailor Soldier Spy*.

The plot of *The Spy Who Came in from the Cold* is significantly more devious than anything Ian Fleming had ever written or, for that matter, anything that le Carré himself had produced before.

Long-time agent Alec Leamas becomes embroiled in a plot, organised by the ubiquitous Control, head of the Circus – but handled, on the fringes, his deputy George Smiley – to force the East Germans to remove one of their leading agents and replace him with another, more amenable character who has already been 'turned' by the British. It is a story of some complexity from which neither side emerges with much credit. As Leamas remarks with bitter sarcasm when talking about the nature of spies and agents:

> What do you think spies are: priests, saints and martyrs? They're a squalid procession of vain fools, traitors too, yes; pansies, sadists and drunkards, people who play cowboys and Indians to brighten their rotten lives ... For God's sake believe me. I hate it, I hate it all; I'm tired. But it's the world, it's mankind, that's gone mad. We're a tiny price to pay.[3]

Cornwell – le Carré as his pseudonym now labelled him – was astounded that the book was passed by both MI5 and MI6 as being appropriate to publish. It was, after all, not a detective story but an espionage tale and was hardly complimentary about the country's espionage services. Dick White, Cornwell's Chief at MI6, was later quite critical of the effect the book had on the reputation of MI6 but at the time of publication, he said nothing.

The public, both British and American, loved the book from the start. It was a case of being the right product at exactly the right moment in time. And when Paramount Pictures made an offer for the film rights, le Carré was finally able to consider becoming a full-time writer.

The film, like the book, was a huge success. Richard Burton gave a stunning performance as Alec Leamas while the black and white cinematography superbly caught the bleakness of the time and the subject matter. In its own way, the film is the equal of the Carol Reed/Graham Greene masterpiece *The Third Man*, being atmospheric, powerful and utterly tragic.

The book was universally hailed as a major success, critics foretelling a bright future for le Carré. However, it did not do the relationship between David and Ann any good whatsoever. If the marriage had been doomed before, now it was as good as over.

***

The Spy Who Came in from the Cold was a 'one-off' creation, a superb 'one-off' it must be admitted, but with Leamas lying dead at the foot of the Berlin Wall, there was no prospect of a sequel. It was in the works which followed that le Carré discovered his real metier.

His experience in the 'hidden world' of spying undoubtedly gave Cornwell/le Carré an advantage over other less experienced writers. For a long while his identity was secret but many suspected that he was writing about a world that he knew only too well and when he was finally 'outed' there was a loud outcry of 'told you so' by many journalists and critics.

In the early 1960s, he finally gave up his job with MI6, a position which had become increasingly irksome to him. At long last le Carré finally became a full-time writer.

There was initially some confusion over his leaving MI6, confusion in which Cornwell in his usual weaving and blending of fact and fiction was happy to wallow. Was he sacked or did he leave voluntarily? The truth, like much of the spying world in which he was involved, lay halfway between the two options.

After the success of his first spy novel, Cornwell/le Carré was told that he could not continue with his formal cover as a diplomat. It was, presumably, a matter of government sensibilities but with the Philby affair still current, it may well be the case that he was too close to reality, both in his fiction and in his personal life. Vacillating as ever, however, MI6 still wanted to retain his services. He was informed that if he wanted to continue with espionage, MI6 could easily arrange a different cover story for him. As a consequence, a number of different options were laid before him.

When faced with the choices, he refused to hide behind the most favoured option, the one that was easiest to set up. That was taking the cover of a journalist. Kim Philby had posed as a writer and journalist and it is possible that le Carré rejected the option on these grounds alone. Whatever the reason, he pressed forward with his intention of leaving government service.

Now that he had been presented with something of a fait accompli, Dick White, head of the organisation, was happy to accept Cornwell's resignation, apparently remarking that le Carré and his fiction had done the secret espionage agencies of Britain no good at all. It was an interesting about-face for MI6 but David Cornwell would probably have regarded it as par for the course.

The successful novelist had moved to Hamburg for the final stage of his espionage career, the move also signalling the beginning of the end for his marriage. It was a time of change, change all round for David Cornwell or John le Carré as he was now being increasingly known, and for his family. And yet there was at least one constant in his life at this time – the compelling, unassuming but totally mesmerising figure of George Smiley.

While not being the central character in *The Spy Who Came in from the Cold*, Smiley still plays an important part in the plot line. As Control's deputy, it is Smiley who handles the complicated mission which ultimately leaves Leamas and Liz, his girlfriend, lying dead on the East German side of the Berlin Wall. The death of the girl is a particularly important issue.

That death, almost more significant than the end of Leamas, is a powerful conclusion to the book. Smiley's first reaction on hearing shots from the Eastern side of the Wall is not, as might be expected, 'What's happened?' but 'Where is the girl, what has happened to the girl?' Many critics have concluded that this final scene is the last act in a complex and convoluted series of betrayals:

> That is the key implication (or so I read it) – that she's never coming over and was never meant to. Leamas suddenly understands this – it is the final betrayal he suffers – and he climbs back down to the East and meets his death.[4]

After it was over, once the book was published, le Carré found that Leamas might be dead but he could not quite let George Smiley go. He was far too good a creation to waste simply as a supporting figure for characters like Alec Leamas and, consequently, he would return time after time in le Carré's masterful drawings of the Secret Service world.

Even for those of us with no knowledge or experience of the secret world of spying, those for whom the espionage novel remains our only contact with agents, double-crosses, moles and the like, George Smiley smacks of reality and realism. This you think – this you know – is how real spies look, speak and act. Smiley's world is filled with rugged, rumbustious secret agents – Jim Prideaux, Peter Guillam and Bill Haydon to name just three – but they are not Smiley.

Smiley is a tireless worker behind the scenes, a plotter and a planner who will carefully research and organise his operations. He is meticulous and hugely efficient, a man who will hold a gun when there is no choice but is more worried about the damage it will cause to the lining of his coat pocket than about the effect it will have if he has to fire the damned thing! Smiley is an academic and a thinker who has somehow found his way into what will always be an alien world for him. He may not like what he does but he knows it is essential for the survival of the world as he knows it.

George Smiley is a remarkable fictional character, a creation that any writer would be proud to own. He appears in nine of le Carré's books, being a central character in five of them, a peripheral – but still important – figure in four more. He is the ubiquitous agent and spy runner, about as far removed from James Bond and other more exotic fictional inventions of the fifties and sixties, as it is humanly possible to be.

***

Following the success of *The Spy Who Came in from the Cold,* John le Carré still found himself embroiled in the world that he knew best – that of spying, double-dealing and trickery. Not doing it or taking part in it any longer, but writing about it.

The crowning achievement of le Carré's writing career has to be the Karla Trilogy – *Tinker Tailor Soldier Spy*, *The Honourable Schoolboy* and *Smiley's People*. The three books stand alone as major contributions to the world of spy fiction. In the hunt for the elusive Soviet spymaster Karla, all three volumes present a united front as Smiley relentlessly tracks down his nemesis, the man who has planted his mole deep inside the Circus. This is betrayal on a grand scale and le Carré, the bit between his teeth, at last, approaches it in grand style.

Bill Haydon, the mole, is a crucial figure in the betrayal and in the first of the three books, not only of Smiley – having slept, on Karla's orders, with his opponent's errant wife – but also his country. The similarity between Haydon and Kim Philby with his unrepentant rejection of the West and its flawed values, displays just how deeply Cornwell was hurt by yet another betrayal in his life. Hurt, yes, but the book would have been so much the poorer without this crucial element to the story.

The plot of *Tinker Tailor Soldier Spy* centres on the hunt for the arch betrayer but further betrayals, albeit less world-shattering ones, come from Smiley's protegees Toby Esterhase and Roy Bland. Both of them, men who have come to work for the Circus as a result of Smiley's influence, have been taken in and are being used by Haydon and Karla as tools to perpetuate the betrayal. Interestingly, only Esterhase returns after the first book in the series. Like Smiley, he is too vital, too interesting a character to ignore.

Karla's influence spreads like a spider's web through all three books. He is rarely seen in the flesh, so to speak, but he still presents as a formidable opponent for Smiley and the men of the Circus. He is omnipresent, an influence on the thoughts and actions of every other character.

Smiley and Karla are different but also frighteningly alike, something which makes their duel compelling reading. The difference between them comes down, eventually, to humanity, too much of it for Smiley, total absence of the emotion for Karla. Only in the Soviet agent's love for his mentally ill daughter – as seen in *Smiley's People* – does some vestige of care and compassion emerge.

At the end of *Smiley's People*, Karla negotiates an about turn and, in the wake of potential exposure, arrest and execution, defects to the West. However, Smiley also demonstrates a total change of heart and attitude. He has endured enough and, like Karla, his is a personal epiphany. After years of betrayal by Ann – the name is significant – he finally confronts his wife before heading off to deal with Karla. In typical Smiley fashion there is no thought or sense of revenge and the episode leaves him unfulfilled and saddened:

> She faced him again and the tears were suddenly running anywhere, worse than before, but they still didn't move him as he wished they would … The tide was out so he walked along the shore near Marazion, scared by his own indifference.[5]

With Karla finally beaten, le Carré felt able to move on to other aspects of the espionage game. With the end of the Cold War, he broadened his scope – as he had, tentatively and perhaps not entirely successfully, done with *The Honourable Schoolboy* – and used his love of travel to explore more exotic climates than the drab brutality of West and East Germany.

He was incapable of writing a bad book but his best late novels, hovering on the fringes of the spy/counterspy world, including *The Little Drummer Girl*, *The Constant Gardener* and perhaps most notable of all, 1993's *The Night Manager*. George Smiley made his penultimate appearance in *The Secret Pilgrim* before making a swan song in one of le Carré's final books, *A Legacy of Spies* (2017).

Over the final twenty or thirty years of his life David Cornwell – as John le Carré – enjoyed huge literary success. He bought himself a strip of cliff-top land in Cornwall, married again and found that whatever he did, wherever he went, he was feted by the literary world. Prizes and honorary degrees flowed his way.

Despite it all, he remained very much an outsider. Adamant in his opinions, he never tolerated lightly those he regarded as fools. He did not just sport singular and heart-felt opinions, he acted on his beliefs.

Adamantly opposed to Britain leaving the European community, Cornwell seized on his distant Irish roots – his father Ronnie came from Irish origins – and in the final years of his life became an Irish citizen. Despite this, he continued to live in England, the country of his birth and which he loved, regardless of what he saw as the stupidity of its leaders.

There was, perhaps, more of Karla than George Smiley in his make-up but that was what made him a seriously great novelist, both within and outside the spy fiction genre. *The Times* newspaper ranked him 22nd in its list of the all-time greatest British writers since 1945, a ranking which many (myself included) feel undervalued his talent and skill.

He died on 12 December 2020 after a fall in his Cornish home. The similarity to the death of John Buchan remains disturbingly obvious. He was 89 years old and his legacy was immense, leaving him, in the opinion of many, to outlive his persona and stand alone as the greatest spy writer ever to put pen to paper.

Chapter Ten

The Triumvirate on the Silver Screen – and More

For many supposed aficionados, it is not just the books produced by The Triumvirate that have made le Carré and the whole spy writing genre so memorable. On the cinema and television screens, not to mention the radio, the stories have morphed into something altogether gripping.

It is, perhaps, symptomatic of the modern age but large numbers of those who queue for hours in wind and rain to see the latest Bond movie may have probably never opened an Ian Fleming book in their lives. That remains something of a shame but it does at least help keep the genre alive.

John Buchan was the first of The Triumvirate to see his work transferred to the cinema screen – more by accident and date of birth than by deliberate policy. By the time Fleming and le Carré were writing their books, cinema and television were well established. Not so in Buchan's days. And, interestingly, it was not, as might have been expected, *The Thirty-Nine Steps* with which he made his screen debut.

Instead, in 1925 *Huntingtower* was made into a silent film, starring the major Scottish comedian and entertainer Harry Lauder. The book was not long out and on the back of this – and Laufer's reputation – the film was a considerable success. That was something not easy to achieve in a film with no dialogue, a medium which at the time was more suited to the antics of Charlie Chaplin and Laurel and Hardy than it was to the romantic drama of John Buchan.

Since then, there have been several small-screen adaptations of *Huntingtower*, notably the 1957 series for children's TV. Starring

James Hayter, this series was shot on location in Scotland and managed to catch the romance of lowland border country as well as maintaining the credibility of Buchan's plot. There was a further TV adaptation produced by BBC Scotland in 1978, starring Paul Curran as Dickson McCunn. Three radio adaptations have also been broadcast over the years.

In 1977 *The Three Hostages* was made into a television series, starring Barry Foster as Richard Hannay. This followed an earlier six-part series broadcast in 1952. But it was with *The Thirty-Nine Steps* that Buchan's work exploded onto the cinema screen.

The 1935 version of the story was directed by Alfred Hitchcock. Despite several flaws, it is a film which has retained its standing and status. It was, for the master of suspense, a perfect vehicle, featuring an innocent man on the run, hunted by police and by his enemies. It was a subject to which Hitchcock returned many times, notably in films like *North by Northwest*.

For his version of *The Thirty-Nine Steps* Hitchcock had to re-write much of Buchan's original book, in particular introducing a female lead to stand alongside Hannay. Robert Donat, already established as one of Britain's leading romantic actors, played a wonderful Richard Hannay and Madeline Carroll his love interest. Although the film was never going to be 100% faithful to the book it is certainly accurate in spirit. Buchan professed himself to be more than happy with the result, feeling that Hitchcock's take on Hannay's dilemma and Donat's portrayal of his main character were more in keeping with modern trends.

Buchan may well have had his tongue in his cheek when he made that remark but the film, then and now, remains hugely enjoyable. In 2004 *Total Film* voted this version of Buchan's book twenty-first in the list of all-time British movies.

A second film version of the book appeared in 1959, Kenneth More giving a light, humorous view of Hannay and the period. Like the first version, this adaptation remained faithful – to

Hitchcock's view of the book rather than Buchan's original. In 1959 More was at the height of his popularity and the film was a huge success.

A third version of *The Thirty-Nine Steps* came out in 1978. It starred Robert Powell as Hannay, John Mills as Scudder, David Warner as a suitably menacing villain and Karen Dotrice as the, by now, essential female character and love interest for Hannay.

The film was full of action and high adventure but was spoiled somewhat by the appearance of a monoplane, bearing an uncanny resemblance to the German Fokker Eindecker fighter of the Great War, firing machine guns through its propellors. Synchronised weapons and forward-firing machine guns did not appear on German fighters until the spring or early summer of 1915 and then on only a limited number. With the film set in the summer of 1914, it was a small anachronism but a mistake nonetheless which spoiled the movie for many Buchan fans.

Despite this minor flaw, the 1978 version was probably closer to the Buchan original than either of the previous adaptations and was followed up by a television series showing Hannay in his pre-1914 role. Again, Robert Powell starred in the TV series but, unfortunately, the idea failed to grab public attention and after the first series the exercise was not repeated.

Yet another version, this time made for the BBC, came out in 2998. Rupert Penry Jones played Hannay and a suitably low-key Patrick Malahide portrayed the villain. Once again there was an anachronism with the aircraft hunting scenes, this time showing a British SE5 fighter – three years before the aeroplane actually went into production!

Following the original Hitchcock film, there had been numerous radio versions of the book, notably with Orson Wells in 1938 and David Niven in 1946. A 'reading' of *The Thirty-Nine Steps*, combined with *Mr Standfast*, was first broadcast by the BBC in 1950 and has since been repeated several times.

Perhaps the most interesting and unusual adaptation of *The Thirty-Nine Steps* came in the comedy/musical stage production which, with a cast of just four playing 139 roles, ran for over 300 performances in the West End. Beginning in 1995 it was the fifth longest-running play in the history of English theatre when the show finally closed in 2015 – not a bad performance when compared with *The Mousetrap* and *Les Misérables* which were also showing in the West End at the time.

When all is said and done the story of Buchan on movie and TV screens is not so much the wonder of what has been filmed but, rather, what has not. *Greenmantle,* the greatest of all his books, has never been made into a movie. Hitchcock was going to turn it into a film but the Buchan estate asked for too much money and the project floundered before it really began. One day, perhaps, one day!

***

The long-lasting series of James Bond films is probably the greatest film franchise of all time. At the time of writing, twenty-five Bond films have appeared from Eon Productions, the Company which owns the franchise, with two more, unconnected movies, making a grand total of twenty-seven films. And there are undoubtedly more to come.

The first of the Bond films hit the cinema screens in 1962. *Dr No* was probably closest to Fleming's original books with Sean Connery playing a wonderful, self-contained hero and Joseph Wiseman an understated but hugely powerful villain. The film provided Ursula Andress with a breakthrough role as Honey Ryder although she had little to do apart from posing in her now-famous white bikini.

The success of *Dr No* confirmed what Producers Albert 'Cubby' Broccoli and Harry Saltzman had always believed – James Bond was going to be a potential gold mine. It was quickly followed by *From Russia with Love* and *Goldfinger,* the two films producing what were probably the best cinematic villains of the whole genre.

Broccoli and Saltzman had formed Eon Productions with the backing of United Artists and now set about procuring the rights to all of Fleming's books. The one title they could not get their hands on was *Casino Royale* which had already been sold to Gregory Ratoff for the 1954 Canadian TV production. The film rights for this particular book duly passed on to Charles Feldmann who, in 1967, produced *Casino Royale* as a spoof Bond film. It was not until well into the twentieth century that Eon was able to make a 'straight' version of Fleming's first book.

The importance of gadgets became increasingly popular as the films were wheeled out, each of the offerings bearing significantly less and less comparison to the original Fleming story. In some cases, it was only the title and a name or two which bore any resemblance to the original book.

The reliance on gadgets was a process that began with Bond's 'hand luggage' in *From Russia with Love* – filled with knives, ammunition and money – and grew steadily more significant with each new film. Perhaps the Aston Martin DB5 that Bond is given by Q Branch in *Goldfinger* remains the most iconic of all these gadgets and devices.

The second non-Eon film was *Never Say Never Again* which was a new version of *Thunderball.* It appeared under a different name as the background to the film was mired in controversy and doubts as to who actually owned the script. Lured back to the role of James Bond, Sean Connery gave his final performance as 007.

Not counting David Niven, who starred in the 1967 comedic version of *Casino Royale*, and discounting the early Canadian TV version, there have been six different actors who have played Bond on the cinema screen. These are Sean Connery, Roger Moore, George Lazenby, Pierce Brosnan, Timothy Dalton and Daniel Craig.

For some time, now, debate has raged as to who made the best Bond but Fleming himself, before his death in 1964, was sure that Connery had caught the character perfectly. At first, he had been unsure about the working-class Scotsman – the very antithesis of Bond, as Fleming wrote him – but, having seen the first film, he quickly changed his mind. He did not live to see what the other actors made of his creation.

***

It was as much television as the big screen cinema adaptations which brought the creations of John le Carré to the wider public notice. There have been many of both but adaptations began with the movie industry.

The Spy Who Came in from the Cold was the first of le Carré's books to be adapted for the cinema screen and was, in the opinion of many, by far the best film version of any of his stories. The film is laden with deceit and depression, the concept of double-cross being available and well-used by forces on both sides of the Iron Curtain. The film perfectly caught the mood of the time, hitting the cinema screens soon after the Cuban Missile Crisis, amidst fears of exactly what was happening on the eastern or Soviet side of the Berlin Wall.

Often overlooked by le Carré aficionados, *Call for the Dead* – le Carré's first book – was produced in 1967 but with a changed name. Filmed and marketed as *The Deadly Affair*, the film starred James Mason as Charles Dobbs, the lead character's name having to be changed from George Smiley because of problems with studio and film rights.

In 2001 *The Tailor of Panama* was made into a film starring one-time Bond actor Pierce Brosnan. It was le Carré stepping outside the borders of Cold War Europe but is now best remembered as the film which gave Harry Potter star Daniel Radcliff his first big acting break.

The Little Drummer Girl was made into a film in 1984 but was not well received, neither by the critics nor by the public. A 2018 BBC television version of the story garnered far better reviews and public appreciation. It followed close on the heels of *The Night Manager* which, in 2016, had proved to be a hugely successful adaptation. This was as much due to Hugh Laurie, everyone's Mr Nice Guy, being cast as the villain of the piece as it was about an admittedly near-perfect storyline.

Several le Carré stories met with a mixed welcome from the public. *A Most Wanted Man* (2014) was largely ignored while *The Looking Glass War* did not receive half of the acclaim it deserved. Other adaptations, such as *The Constant Gardener* which gave Rachel Weisz an Oscar, were critically lauded by everyone.

However, it was the 1970s television adaptations of two of le Carré's Karla books, *Tinker Tailor Soldier Spy* and *Smiley's People*, that really propelled le Carré into public notice and sent George Smiley soaring into the stratosphere as everyone's ideal of the incongruous spymaster. Alec Guinness played the part to perfection, being surrounded by dozens of quality actors who are often overlooked in the acclaim thrown at Guinness. Patrick Stewart, who speaks not a word in either adaptation, presents as a wonderfully menacing Karla.

A big screen film version of *Tinker Tailor Soldier Spy* came out in 2011. Despite being popular with the critics and the public, it inevitably suffered in comparison to the TV series which, by the nature of the medium, was able to devote more time to character development. Gary Oldman was nominated for an Oscar for his performance as Smiley and le Carré/Cornwell even made a cameo appearance in the Christmas party scene in the film.

Over a dozen le Carré books have been adapted for the screen. One of the most significant aspects of those adaptations, be they for television or the cinema, is that they remain relatively faithful to the original story – not something that can be said about the film and

The Triumvirate on the Silver Screen – and More

TV versions of books by John Buchan and Ian Fleming. If nothing else that fact speaks wonders for the dramatic and visual power of le Carré's writing.

***

Apart from the three members of The Triumvirate, several other espionage writers have had their work adapted for the cinema and television.

Perhaps most notable amongst these are Graham Greene, Eric Ambler, Len Deighton and Frederick Forsyth – although even Erskine Childers' *Riddle of the Sands* has now found its way onto the silver screen. Clearly, the spy story has proved to be both durable and entertaining and, on a personal level, I can see no reason why this should change.

Greene's *Our Man in Havana* starring Alec Guinness long before his George Smiley days, was a huge success at the Box Office. So, too, were a number of Eric Ambler's stories, notably the 1943 version of *Journey into Fear*. This starred Joseph Cotton and Orson Welles, the same duo that later achieved such success with Greene's *The Third Man*.

Television in particular has proved to be a perfect vehicle for the spy story. The 1960s and 70s saw a plethora of espionage series, everything from *Callan* and *The Professionals* to *The Prisoner* and *Spooks*. It is a trend which still continues:

> Spy fiction has long been regarded as excellent material
> for films, but the golden age of this genre brought the spy
> story into the living-rooms via the television screen.[1]

Interestingly, the world of spy novels has remained something of a male-dominated genre. Given that some of the greatest real-life spies, particularly during the Cold War period, have been women, the reason for this remains something of a mystery. Even gripping TV programmes like *Vigil,* while featuring two women as lead characters, was written by a man. It is hard to know why this male dominance should have come about, particularly when women do turn their hands to spy fiction their work is invariably both masterful and gripping.

Perhaps the greatest or most effective female spy writers are Helen MacInnes, Stella Rimington – one-time Director General of MI5 – and Stephanie Meyer. Unfortunately, none of their books has yet been turned into a film or TV series although Rimington's Liz Carlyle series would seem to be perfectly pitched for exactly that type of adaptation.

Outside The Triumvirate, Len Deighton's Harry Palmer was perhaps the most successful spy to make it onto cinema screens. Starring Michael Caine, three of Deighton's books, *The Ipcress File, Funeral in Berlin* and *Bullet to Beijing*, were made into hugely successful movies along with two others – *Midnight in St Petersburg* and *Billion Dollar Brain* – that were original screenplays and not based on Deighton books at all. In March 2022 a six-part television adaptation of *The Ipcress File*, starring Joe Cole who had made his name in the TV drama series *Peaky Blinders*, was shown on ITV.

Interestingly, and as an aside, Jason Connery, son of Bond actor Sean Connery, appeared in two of the Harry Palmer films alongside Michael Caine. He also starred in the 1990 film *Spy-maker: The Secret Life of Ian Fleming*, a rather loosely based version and dramatization of the wartime career of the Bond creator.

***

With the death of John le Carré, the last of the three, The Triumvirate has now passed into history. Their work remains a lasting tribute to their skill and while they will not be able to produce more books and stories, there are other writers waiting to replace them at the forefront of espionage writing.

The style of spy writing will, inevitably, change in the years ahead. There will probably be more emphasis on the technology of spying. That is only to be expected. I only hope that this does not spoil the essential ingredients of the spy story – good characters, good locations and good plots to be worked through to a suitable conclusion.

One thing remains abundantly clear. If those basic elements are adhered to, the spy story, in whatever format or style the writers might choose, will remain as one of the most popular genres of writing.

Notes

Chapter One

1. Donald McCormick, *Who's Who in Spy Fiction*, Sphere, p. 10
2. Baroness Emmuska Orczy, *The Scrap of Paper*, quoted on www.goodreads.com
3. Erskine Childers, *The Riddle of the Sands*, Sidgwick & Jackson, p. 198
4. Phil Carradice, *A Hundred Years of Spying*, Pen & Sword, p. 30

Chapter Two

1. Ursula Buchan, *Beyond the Thirty-Nine Steps*, Bloomsbury, p. 10
2. Janet Adam Smith, *John Buchan and His World*, Thames and Hudson, p. 7
3. John Buchan, writing in Hutchesonian Magazine, quoted in 'Beyond the Thirty-Nine Steps'
4. John Buchan, *Memory Hold the Door*, Hodder & Stoughton, p. 13
5. Ibid, pp. 47-48

Chapter Three

1. Janet Adam Smith, p. 42
2. John Buchan, *Memory Hold the Door*, pp. 111-112
3. Janet Adam Smith, p. 52
4. Ibid, p. 56

5. John Buchan, Dedication in *The Thirty-Nine Steps*, Longmans, p. 5
6. Donald McCormick, p. 45
7. John Buchan, *Memory Hold the Door*, p. 169

Chapter Four

1. James Buchan, *Forward to Greenmantle*, Capuchin Classics, p. 12
2. Janet Adam Smith, p. 75
3. James Buchan, Ibid, p. 11
4. John Buchan, *Sick Heart River*, Polygon, p. 192
5. Donald McCormick, Ibid, p. 14
6. Ibid, p. 111
7. Ibid, p. 168

Chapter Five

1. Quoted in John Pearson, *The Life of Ian Fleming*, p. 12
2. Ibid, John Pearson, p. 26
3. Ian Fleming, *Thrilling Cities*, Vintage, p. 221

Chapter Six

1. John Pearson, pp. 92-93
2. Quoted in John Pearson, p. 115

Chapter Seven

1. John Pearson, pp. 205-206
2. Ian Fleming, *Casino Royale*, Vintage, p. 1
3. Alan Judd, Introduction to *Casino Royale*, Vintage, p. X
4. Ian Fleming, Ibid, p. 229
5. www.wikipedia.org/wiki.Ian-Fleming

6. Quoted in publisher's blurb for *Casino Royale*, Vintage, 2012
7. Jeremy Black, article 'The World of James Bond,' *Rowman Now*, Issue 1, p. 8
8. Donald McCormick, p. 93
9. Ian Fleming, *Casino Royale*, p. 208
10. Paul Johnson, article 'Sex, Snobbery and Sadism,' in *New Statesman*, 2021
11. James Fleming, article in *Literary Review*, December 2021, p. 80
12. Michael Wood, article 'James Bond's Place in British Culture,' p. 10, in *BBC History Today*, December 2021
13. William Cook, article in *New Statesman*, p. 40, June 2004

Chapter Eight

1. Donald McCormick, p. 14
2. Quoted in *John le Carré*, Adam Sisman, Bloomsbury, p. X1V
3. www.wikipedia.org/John_le_Carré
4. John le Carré, *The Pigeon Tunnel*, p. 3

Chapter Nine

1. Adam Sisman, p. 217
2. Ibid, p. 232
3. John le Carré, *The Spy Who Came in From the Cold*, Penguin Modern Classics, p. 244
4. John le Carré, '*Smiley's People*, Sceptre, p. 304
5. William Boyd, Introduction to *Tinker, Tailor, Soldier, Sailor*, 2010 edition, p. X11

Chapter Ten

1. Donald McCormick, p. 18

Bibliography

Books consulted in the writing of this book

Books by The Triumvirate

John Buchan
: *Greenmantle*
Huntingtower
Memory Hold the Door
Mr Standfast
Prester John
Sick Heart River
The Thirty-Nine Steps

Ian Fleming
: *Casino Royale*
Dr No
Goldfinger
Live and Let Die
Thrilling Cities
Thunderball

John le Carré
: *A Perfect Spy*
Call for the Dead
The Pigeon Tunnel
The Spy Who Came in From the Cold
Tinker Tailor Soldier Spy
The Honourable Schoolboy
Smiley's People

Books by Other Writers

Anon, *The Book of Bond or Every Man His Own 007*, Pan, London, 1965

Eric Ambler, *Journey into Fear*, Pan, London, 1999 (reprint)

William Amos, *Who's Really Who in Fiction*, Sphere, London, 1987

Ursula Buchan, *Beyond the Thirty-Nine Steps*, Bloomsbury, London, 2019

Phil Carradice, *A Hundred Years of Spying*, Pen & Sword, Barnsley, 2021

Gordon Corera, *MI6: Life and Death in the British Secret Service*, Weidenfeld & Nicolson, London, 2012

Erskine Childers, *The Riddle of the Sands*, Sidgwick & Jackson, London, 1927

Hugh and Graham Greene, (editors) *The Spy's Bedside Book*, Arrow Books, London, 2007

Phillip Knightley, *The Second Oldest profession*, Norton, London, 1986

William Le Queux, *If England Were Invaded*, Bodleian Library, Oxford, 2014

Donald McCormick, *Who's Who in Spy Fiction*, Sphere, London, 1979

John Pearson, *The Life of Ian Fleming*, Bloomsbury, London, 2013

Oleg Penkovsky, *The Penkovsky Papers*, Fontana, London, 1965

Adam Sisman, *John le Carré*, Bloomsbury, London, 2016

Janet Adam Smith, *John Buchan and his World*, Thames & Hudson, London, 1979

Web Pages

www.wikipedia.org/John_le_Carré
www.wikipedia.org/wiki.Ian-Fleming
www.goodreads.com

Magazines

New Statesman, June 2004 and December 2021
Literary Review, August 2021
BBC History Today, December 2021
BBC History, 2020-to date
Rowman Now, Issue No 1